Creative and Philosophical Thinking in Primary Schools

Teach to Inspire

www.teachingexpertise.com/teachtoinspire

Creative and Philosophical Thinking in Primary Schools

Marie Huxtable, Ros Hurford
and Joy Mounter

A catalogue record of this book is available from the British Library.

This book is commissioned by Barbara Maines and George Robinson for Teach to Inspire, a series for Optimus Education.

Authors:

Marie Huxtable, Ros Hurford, Joy Mounter

Designer:

Jess Wright

Editors:

Barbara Maines and George Robinson

Copy Editor:

Mel Maines

Printed by: Hobbs the Printers Ltd.

Registered Office: Brunel Road, Totton, Hampshire SO40 3WX

Registered Number: 422 132

Published by Optimus Education: a division of Optimus Professional Publishing Ltd.

Registered Office: 33-41 Dallington Street, London EC1V 0BB

Registered Number: 05791519

Telephone: 0845 450 6407 Fax: 0845 450 6410

www.teachingexpertise.com

ISBN 978-1-906517-09-0

Contents

Acknowledgements

We would like to say thank you for the patient and gentle help and support of Moira Laidlaw, Barbara Maines and George Robinson. We would also like to say how much we owe to the creative and philosophical thinking and the good humoured energy of the children we have worked with and the Tuesday Masters group at the University of Bath, with whom we have shared so much of our learning journey over the last few years.

We would particularly like to thank Claire Formby, Nina Clayton, Meg White, Amy Skuze, Sally Cartwright, Louise Cripps and Vicky Tucker for sharing their accounts and stories. Last, but not least, we would like to acknowledge the inspiring presence in this book of Belle Wallace, Jack Whitehead and the late Kate St John; long may their educational influence flourish.

Foreword

What I find most refreshing about this book is the way in which three educators, with many years of experience, show their professional and personal commitment to each other and to the children in their care. With the national and global interest in enhancing professionalism in education we have a text that shows how this can be done with a focus on creative and philosophical thinking for children.

The book is practical, showing clearly how creative and philosophical thinking can be developed in the everyday classroom. We are taken directly into educational relationships with children and the creative responses of the teachers to their pupils' needs. We are shown the insights the authors draw on from various approaches and theories. Rather than just being applied as a fixed framework these insights are used creatively and with philosophical reflection in supporting the thinking of the pupils.

The emphasis on values is also significant. I know that we cannot distinguish anything as educational without affirming that it is of value. It is, however, unusual to see values being affirmed so clearly. It is also unusual to see educators providing accounts of how they are seeking to live their values as fully as they can in their practice. This is what makes the text of such practical use. We are taken inside the living experience of educators and shown how they are trying to improve what they are doing from the inside of their practice. They are not offering templates for others to use; they are offering their explanations of the educational influences of their own learning and in the learning of children. They are offered as gifts for you to use as you will in the development of your own unique responses to the contexts and relationships you are working in.

While practical, the book is also profoundly theoretical in the sense that it shows three educators explaining what they are doing in terms of their values. We are shown the values that explain why they are doing what they are doing in emphasising the importance of creative and philosophical thinking. We are shown the different theoretical perspectives and personal experiences that have helped to form their unique contributions to education. With the national and global interest in enhancing professionalism in education, the three educators have shown how a profession of master educators could easily be created from within the embodied knowledge of the profession itself. In this book Joy Mounter, Rosalind Hurford and Marie Huxtable show how the embodied knowledge of educators can be made public through narratives that include explanations of educational influences in learning.

I think that you will enjoy seeing how the educators use the systematic approach to their educational enquiries known as Thinking Actively in a Social Context (TASC). This action research approach was developed by Belle Wallace (2001) while working in KwaZulu-Natal. It embodies a cyclical approach in which the individual asks: What do I know about this? What is the task? How many ideas can I think of? What is the best idea? Let's do it! How well did I do? Let's tell someone! What have I learned?

What is most exciting to me about this action research approach to learning is that it can be used by 6 year olds, by the educators producing this text and by me, a 64-year-old educator and educational researcher. Through following the evolution of the three educators' own creative and philosophical thinking and in helping young people to develop their own, we are shown the value of using TASC in the enhancement of learning.

I shall continue to revisit this text, especially the narratives in which the three educators reveal the most significant influences on their values. I feel privileged when individuals share what matters most to them in their professional lives. I also feel revitalised when I experience the sustained and sustaining passion of other educators for the values I associate with carrying hope for the future of humanity and my own. If these pages evoke a similar response in you to those in me we may find that they stimulate us to contribute our own stories, of the evolution of our creative and philosophical thinking in our educational relationships with our pupils and students, to our professional knowledge-base of education.

Jack Whitehead,

Lecturer in Education, University of Bath

Visiting Professor, Ningxia Teachers University, China.

Part 1
The Background

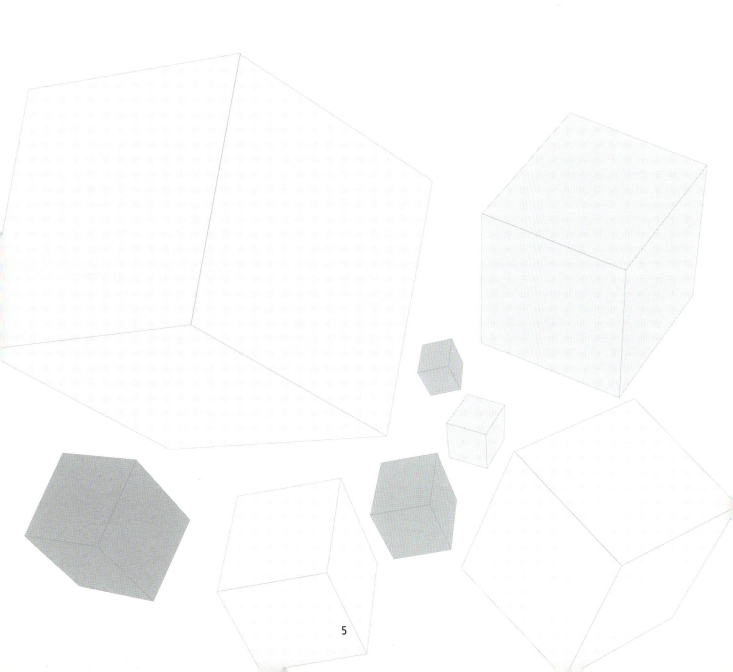

Chapter 1
Introduction

We, Ros, Joy and Marie, are always trying to find better ways to help our children grow educationally and retain our own enthusiasm for our work in education. Although we have pursued different paths we have, over the years, come to realise the importance of creative and philosophical thinking as expressions of our educational values and intentions. We have developed our own understandings of what is important to us, tested, reflected, changed and modified what we do, revised and developed our explanations of why we do what we do, and recognised the values that drive us.

We will tell you about some of our journeys so you might understand what we are trying to do and why. We describe something of the culture, attitudes, skills and understandings we are trying to develop with our pupils and some of the moments, activities and ideas that we can identify that 'worked' for us. It is work in progress as we, like our pupils, are forever learning, with the intention that what we do tomorrow will be better than what we do today. We hope that some of our stories will resonate with you and you might find something which challenges or affirms your own practice and theories, provokes a new thought or offers you something to experiment with.

Our journeys have not been neatly planned on smooth, straight paths, in idyllic settings always meeting with success. We do our best in the real world. We stumble, go round in circles, stray up exciting blind alleys, enter the pits, have selective memories and benefit from hindsight.

We will start by describing our evolving ideas and practices of creative and philosophical thinking and then, in Part 2, give you some detail about why we see it as important, how to get going, and suggest some ideas on how you might want to develop it further.

As you read our book, dip in and out, go to the back and work to the middle, whatever suits you. We encourage you to create your own rationale for why you want to develop creative and philosophical thinking in your classrooms, and refine, revise and create your own theories and practices.

We hope to engage you in creative and philosophical thinking with us. We hope this will embolden you and stimulate your imaginations to go beyond the pages of this book into your classrooms and lives, to research your own practice, create your own living educational theory and share your ideas with others so we can all progress. As Victor Quinn (1997) wrote:

> 'There is a quality even more fundamental than the truth in your ideas, and that is that they are your ideas. You owe it to the group that the ideas be heard. They deserve to have their go, to have their chance in the world and their chance in our group. So whatever reluctance there is on your part to contribute to the group, and for whatever reason, it must be overcome, for your sake and for the ideas' sake. Do not feel exonerated by the fact that you can gain much from a discussion by just listening. Others should be able to benefit from you as you can from then. What sort of group member and colleague are you if you not only don't but can't readily put your views and experience to a group?'

Chapter 2
Creative and Philosophical Thinking and their Evolution in our Practise

'Children have this capacity to open me up to the universe inside their heads and see everything in more alive ways. This is why I find teaching is the best job in the world.'

Moira Laidlaw

Reading this Book

We believe we have an educational responsibility to enable our pupils to learn how to recognise the people they are and want to be, to grow in their understanding of a world worth living in and how they might contribute by learning to live their lives as well as they can. It is easy to lose sight of our educational principles with the relentless demand to train children in the tool skills of literacy and numeracy and the incessant demand to 'raise standards'. We believe the skills of creative and philosophical thinking are so important educationally that we do not want them to become yet another set of dissociated skills. At the same time we are aware that they can be enhanced by engaging our children in opportunities to learn them.

Creative and philosophical thinking are intimately inter-related in the story of developing our educational practice. Sometimes we have devised activities specifically to develop one form of thinking or another, but for the most part, it is often hard to see where one begins and the other ends. However, to make our story easier to follow we describe activities and approaches we have tried with particular purposes in mind that we have come to recognise as organising principles, developing:

- playful and experimental thinking outside the box
- the ability of the children to pose questions that are important to them and create answers which are reasoned and reasonable
- the children's awareness and appreciation of themselves and others as knowledge creators
- the children's confidence and ability to challenge their own thinking and the status quo
- the children's ability to create options for themselves within constraints and to be open to opportunities.

In the last section we bring these together with the 'higher' organising principles, researching to improve our understanding of ourselves, and the contribution we make to the world:

- Children learning to research to contribute to their world.
- Children learning to learn about themselves.
- Walking the talk – teachers researching to understand and improve their own practice.

In the final chapter we share with you our own evolving stories of our thinking which have emerged as we have written this book.

We will introduce you to the meanings we give to creative and philosophical thinking through snapshots and commentaries on what we have tried and the way our methods developed. This is designed to illustrate the sort of responses you might get from your pupils and where some of the connections with the rest of the educational experiences you provide for them might be made. For the most part, in practice, we have found it is difficult and unhelpful to try to pigeonhole a session as 'creative' or 'philosophical'; it is more useful to focus on explaining to you why we are doing what we are doing. Through this we hope you will understand the attitudes, attributes, skills and understandings we are trying to nurture and then be able to reflect on whether that requires an emphasis on one type of thinking or another. For instance, Chapter 2 concerns playful and experimental thinking, but you can see how this includes elements that range from creative to more philosophical thinking. In the same way, attitudes, attributes, skills and understandings are not discrete. They overlap and intertwine in places, producing a fascinating range of combinations. Just as the citizenship curriculum touches that of history, so becoming self-reflective is not unrelated to developing an awareness and appreciation of others.

You may prefer not to follow a linear path and instead meander back and forth and develop your own ideas with snippets of the text to provoke, inform and challenge. We will often talk to you with our combined voices but we will also talk with our individual voice and then we will introduce the speaker, to enable you to recognise who you are talking with. While we share much of our thinking and have ideas that frequently overlap, we are individuals with different professional experiences who at times have distinct perspectives and insights to offer. If you find some inconsistencies in what we talk about, it is because we value learning that comes through opportunities to argue constructively. We accept that we can each come to a reasoned and reasonable answer which may not be the same as someone else's and indeed we may change our minds as we continue to inquire.

We also want to share with you some of our own thinking and explanations of why we do what we do and why it is important to us. In this way we hope you too will come to understand the value of these activities in your own practice and begin, enthusiastically, your own journey to extend creative and philosophical thinking. Each of us has followed an individual route, but we hope our preceding experiences will help you along the way. At every dead end or wrong turning in our experiences we have been guided by the overriding conviction that creative and philosophical thinking is not just for childhood, it's for life!

Creative and Philosophical Thinking: What do we Mean and Why are they Important?

Creative and philosophical thinking are not separate areas with definite boundaries, nor are they separated from the thinking needed to make significant progress in creating knowledge in identified fields such as science or art, or even to making progress through the National Curriculum. However, they are distinguishable from much of the thinking described in the curriculum materials by the purpose which we have for developing them in the educational environment of our schools and classrooms.

We want our pupils to experience the pleasure we have experienced that comes from allowing our own creative spark to be fanned into life and to voyage to uncharted places intellectually. We want children to grow with a love of learning, to delight in engaging in the learning process to acquire new knowledge, to develop wisdom and sometimes to give themselves permission to just have fun and play cognitively.

We want our pupils to be emancipating influences in their own learning and their own lives, so they value themselves and what they create, and extend their confidence and ability to develop as in(ter)dependent people with an ability to live lives they feel are satisfying, productive and worthwhile, contributing to the wellbeing and well-becoming of us all.

To give a single definition is impossible. There are more definitions out there than you have had targets and tests. However you are welcome to try and we would be interested to hear from you if you would like to tell us where your thinking takes you. We think you might find the actual process of coming to your own answers more use than the sentences you eventually come up with. In doing this you will have experienced something of what we mean by the sort of creative and philosophical thinking this book is about. For each of us it is a unique understanding and experience. Words can begin to describe it but, like the story of the blind men and the elephant, we all have our own perceptions and interpretations, all different but sharing common threads.

So, let us start at the end. What do we mean by creative and philosophical thinking? Our understanding and practice are evolving, influenced by our experiences and the activities we develop for the children, but also through discussing our ideas, writing this book and continuing to research our practice to improve it. We meet you at a point in that evolution, and welcome you to join in its future progress.

Creative thinking is the sort of thinking that you do when you are enjoying the pleasure of your own originality, creating and co-creating new knowledge, playing with ideas, experimenting, experiencing the thrill of intellectually venturing forth on previously un-trod paths, following your curiosity and imagination, creating your dreams… It is the sort of thinking where you unexpectedly come across fun in thoughts. The human ability to think the previously unimagined and act towards that evolving vision, is what has moved us from the world of our ancestors who were at the mercy of their circumstances. We evolve our world and ourselves as we create both.

Philosophical thinking is the sort of thinking that enables you to create and explore, with increasing sophistication and expertise, questions about what matters to you, your life, the life you want to live, the world you want to live in, the society you want to be a part of, what it is that gives meaning and purpose to your existence. If you think this might be way over the heads of your pupils we hope to disabuse you of that notion. It is these big questions that very young children are able to ask and answer with a passion and enthusiasm that schooling and adults extinguish, unless we are very careful.

'One had to cram all this stuff into one's mind for the examinations, whether one liked it or not. This coercion had such a deterring effect on me that, after I had passed the final examination, I found the consideration of any scientific problems distasteful to me for an entire year.'

Albert Einstein

It is as well that Einstein survived his education!

We believe that providing the opportunity and support for children to develop their creative and philosophical thinking is of vital importance in providing them with an education that will enable them to understand the world they live in, make sense of the information and skills they need to live fulfilled lives and help them to see that learning is pleasurable, personal and contributes to improving the world for all of us. Each learning journey is different but we hope one of our stories resonates with you and helps you reflect on your own teaching practices and think about the evolution of your own, and your pupils', creative and philosophical thinking.

The Evolution of our Thinking and Practice

Ros's Account

I wonder if you've ever considered the answers to any of the following questions:

- Do plants get fat?
- Do we evaporate out in the sun on a hot day?
- If angels live in the sky, why can't we see them when we're in a plane?
- Will the world end?
- Is getting what you need the same as getting what you want?
- What would happen if all the animals on the planet died?

Up to about ten years ago they had never crossed into my adult consciousness. I lived a happy and fulfilled life without them to worry about. 'Real' life posed enough questions of its own without inventing any. Moreover, they weren't the type of questions I saw much purpose to. Adults thought 'serious' and 'important' thoughts. Musing over the inner secrets of plant life was something I had left behind in childhood, or rather I assumed I had.

Today this is far from the case. Recently I spent a good ten minutes discussing with a ten year old why, if the earth rotates at a fairly rapid rate, we do not feel the movement. It didn't involve me telling the child about how we deal with this. Rather it was more a sharing of the wonder that, given we were participants in this rotation, we didn't feel dizzy.

This sense of wonder at the world is a crucial element to the work I do with the children in my class. It is the aspect of teaching that still, after over 20 years, makes me passionate about what I do. Thinking creatively and outside the box is exciting. I can find no other way to describe it. There's a tingle that a new original way of looking at a problem or situation can bring. This excitement for learning is what I am trying to foster in the children. It was there when they were very small and I see it as an important part of my job to keep its flame burning for as long as I can.

In the Beginning

I want to take you back to those points I can remember as the start of developing creative and philosophical thinking in my classroom. My intention is to tell you the story of how it evolved and became an area of fascination and importance to me. My wish is that you will be reassured that it began with no special training or local authority funded course. There was no handbook to follow, no assessment sheet to fill in. It just grew into a way of working and thinking that I have grown to love and value highly. It is the story of my own learning journey and enlightenment.

For several years now I have been teaching full-time at a local junior school. During that time I have moved year groups, taken on different areas of responsibility and seen many organisational changes. My pupils are lovely, very open, straight talking and a delight to work with. They are sometimes referred to as 'challenging'. Many do not enjoy the benefits of materially comfortable homes and school can be seen as a place where their parents and extended families did not experience success. For a few, school is a place where they feel they belong and are offered opportunities and consistency. They are not always easy children to teach. Frequently, problems in the classroom are a consequence of children not having had enough sleep, not having read to anyone at home or not doing their homework. The content of the National Curriculum is only of minor importance or relevance to many of them.

How can I Make the Children More Involved in their Own Learning?

Learning journeys often begin with a problem to solve, and in my case this was, 'How can I make the children more involved in their own learning?' I wanted to increase their self-motivation to learn, not just stop if they got to the end of the task I had given them. We often discussed in the staffroom how wonderful it would be to have a magic wand in reserve which, with one wave, we could transform a class into a bright-eyed bunch of eager learners! What I didn't realise at the beginning was that the magic of motivation and curiosity was there in every child and all I had to do was adapt my teaching methods to release it.

I was an established, experienced teacher and felt increasingly dissatisfied with what was happening in my classroom. I began to realise that if I churned out the same type of teaching methods I would get the same responses. The responses I was getting were leading me to assume that the situation was hopeless and it was stupid to expect more from these children. It was during this time of professional 'frustration' that those original questions arose, leading me to reflect more carefully on the whole complicated area of learning and how I could introduce changes in my practice to increase the motivation and interest of the children. My starting point was acknowledging a problem and making myself open to creating a solution. The way forward came as I developed solutions through a blend of my creative thinking and philosophy.

Starting to Think

My journey largely began with 'creative thinking'. My own use of the term covers problem-solving and investigating 'what if' situations, where a conventional solution is not available and imaginative responses have to be brought into play. Many of the situations I use are totally unreal or unlikely, such as travelling by broomstick or exploring an alien planet. Activities such as these are great fun and they have no boundaries of reality to limit them. This use of the imagination is very important in developing as a learner in the classroom and for life. For instance, allowing his imagination to flow unimpeded triggered Einstein's theories. According to the American Museum of Natural History, when he was just 16 years old, Einstein tried to imagine what it would be like to ride on a beam of light. Could he travel as fast as light? Could he travel faster? In 1905, nearly a decade after this first 'thought experiment', Einstein answered these questions with his Special Theory of Relativity.

I have found many of the influential voices in education also stress the importance of creative thinking. Being able to refer to them has helped me feel more confident when I talk to colleagues so I have kept a note of useful references. For instance, this one from Guy Claxton (2001), 'In the learner's toolkit imagination is the ability to sense and feel situations which are not physically present, and to explore how they might behave and develop in the mind's eye… The ability to "go to the movies in your head" is one of the most powerful learning tools we possess.'

Linked closely to the creative thinking activities I provide, which I think of as activities through which children can create practical responses to hypothetical situations, is the area I call 'philosophy'. This is when I encourage the children to participate in discussions and inquiries. These are mainly verbal activities.

Were you to observe either of these sessions you would easily recognise which were taking place, and yet there is a common theme to them in that they both require dealing with situations, which are not there in the present moment. I think Robert Fisher (2003) puts it well when he says, 'Philosophy for children encourages the search for creative options, different viewpoints and ways of thinking.'

The questions I began with, such as, 'Do plants get fat?' have no one single answer. There is no accepted 'truth' that will fit them, but they are fascinating to discuss. They came, seemingly out of the blue, from children in my class. With hindsight I'm inclined to think that questions like them had been around all the time, and as a child I had probably asked similar ones, but there's a tendency for life to dull the curiosity. Mathew Lipmann (2003) suggests that much of our curiosity about life is squeezed out when we start formal education, which is rather ironic seeing that education is supposed to be about learning what we need for life. Yet, walk through town on a busy day, drop in at the swimming pool or catch a bus, and you will hear interesting questions being asked all the time from small children, generally to the exasperation of the adult with them: Why do traffic lights have those colours? What makes puddles disappear? How does our skin grow?

Creating Opportunity in the National Curriculum

My purpose here is to tell you how I found ways to adapt parts of the National Curriculum to a more creative thinking approach. I believe that if you, like me, let yourself be open to taking a slightly different perspective on what you already do, then there is nothing to stop the same sense of adventure, possibility and pleasure entering your work with children and incorporating more creativity in your teaching. I know that no two schools are identical, so your solutions will be different to mine. I haven't found year groups or children to be identical either but creative thinking has enabled me to adapt activities and questions to the group I am working with at the time.

The National Curriculum provides a framework of skills and subjects deemed desirable for the population to learn about; it does not begin with what the child thinks and feels is interesting about the world. As adults we grow into dealing with the practical aspects of existence and perhaps become too accepting of dominant opinions and ideas. Fortunately, for some reason, at that time, my sense of curiosity was rekindled. I have never looked back. Maybe my curiosity had become as dulled by a prescriptive curriculum as that of the children.

The original questions were very much linked to science. The science curriculum often throws up more interesting 'other' questions than the objectives listed in the Qualifications and Curriculum Authority (QCA) documents. Picking up on these as a way of developing creative thinking with the children does not stop them studying the required important facts and skills; rather the questions can enhance their understanding and encourage them to retain their natural curiosity about the world.

We had been studying life processes – what plants and animals need and do. Chris was a boy in my class who produced an average effort in science but never really gave you the impression of enjoying or really understanding it much. He was one of those children who would probably get a comment such as, 'Needs to link scientific facts to his observations,' on his report and just scrape an average grade.

At the end of one lesson, when we were clearing up, Chris asked me about plants getting fat. For a moment I was seriously thrown. I'd never thought about it, but there was something quirky enough in the question to demand I considered it now and in this I was joined by a few other children. Chris's theory was that if humans and animals (such as his nan's dog) got fat from eating more than their bodies needed, then why didn't plants get fat when they had plenty of nourishment in the soil and lots of rain and sun. It's a reasonable enough stance to take if you think about it.

We chewed over some ideas and came up with a variety of theories, but there was little time to pursue the matter further that day. It could have remained dead in the water, except the idea of a fat plant fascinated me. More than this, I think it made me look at Chris in a new light and wonder if there was a lot more going on in his head than I had previously given him credit for. I thought, if this was true for him, what about the other children? Was I so busy teaching the objectives from the official curriculum that I had lost sight of what twists and turns learning could sometimes take?

Being Open to Possibilities

I have this theory (and it is only my theory) that when you leave yourself open in life to anything being possible, then the strangest 'coincidences' happen. A few weeks later I was at a maths course and we were just chatting over coffee, getting to know each other and asking about the subjects we had trained in. One of the teachers there had started out as a secondary science teacher. Well, nothing ventured, nothing gained, so I asked him about Chris's question. He didn't smile one of those weak polite smiles or move to another table, instead he spent coffee break explaining to me how a plant or tree will channel the extra nutrition into growing more branches or leaves. So, in a way, plants do respond to overeating but without the need for Weight Watchers or going to the gym. This for me was a fascinating thought; plants with a more efficient method of dealing with excess – and of course the picture started to form of fully grown large oaks down at the gym lifting weights.

There it was, the beginning of something new; a different way of questioning things that were familiar and I thought I understood. No great fanfare or explosion, no sense of 'eureka', but from that time there was a definite change in how I approached things in my own personal life and also my professional work. The two are hard to separate and I would urge you not to worry about whether you need to develop your thinking first, or whether you let your thinking develop as you encourage the children to do so.

I get the odd looks, some comments about being a bit quirky, but what goes on in my head and the responses I have had from children have been far more interesting than run-of-the-mill stuff. I use different ways of dealing with these responses. Describing myself as a lateral thinker or able to 'think outside the box' are useful ploys. By encouraging children to retain their creativity I am opening up their learning capabilities and increasing my own.

The desirability of being creative is becoming far more accepted as we move towards a future that we can no longer begin to imagine so there are more people I can refer to if necessary, like this quotation from Edward De Bono (2007), 'Everyone should want to be more creative. Creativity makes life more fun, more interesting and more full of achievement.'

I would ask you to remember that back at the start I travelled in optimistic hope without any view of a map. This I refer to as 'Zen travel' – working intuitively and being open to pleasant surprises or rethinking unexpected results. This is really what much of teacher practitioner research is like. I become aware of a problem and look for solutions; some work, others are discarded or modified, but it's largely incorporated into my daily life with no grand scheme or plan worked out in advance.

Some of what I have developed has been founded on the theory and practice offered by others. The ideas I have tried have by no means been solely of my own invention and there are several influences in developing my practice that I remain indebted to. One of these was an introduction to using 'Bloom's Taxonomy' to improve the questions I asked. It remains firmly fixed in my memory in the image of a red chrysanthemum, as I had never heard of Bloom or taxonomy I somehow made a gardening connection. The image is not entirely wasted. Learning involves a lot of patience, not seeing the end result immediately, and requires nurturing.

Up to that point I had never considered the different nature of questions, except that I knew I preferred the interesting, complicated ones to the simple ones. Bloom's Taxonomy (1956) is worth a look at if you want to put your questioning into categories, or you want to check that you are asking a wide and varied type of question (page 142). However I found it more useful to read and really get to grips with what it meant to me rather than keeping a checklist to tick off. By making sure that I ask higher order questions as well as the simpler ones of comprehension, I challenge the children to think creatively and philosophically in curriculum focused sessions.

I have found the responses of the children very rewarding and it has helped them to be more self-motivating. This is where I began to realise the practical implications of researching my own practice. As Robert Fisher (2003) points out, classroom research and giving children intellectually stimulating things to do supports students to become better motivated and more engaged in classes. Both the teacher and children developing higher order questioning is part of those processes.

Following this, my headteacher introduced me to the work of Howard Gardner (1984) on multiple intelligences and suggested that this might be worth incorporating into my practice. This was another influence that made me feel that there was educational value beyond personal pleasure in what I was doing. Again, this is something that has gained general popularity in schools and brought changes in teaching methods into the classroom, but back then this was powerful new information for me. I began to be more aware initially of my different strengths as a learner and from this followed a curiosity about the way my pupils learn, their preferred approach and how these need to be addressed in the classroom. It was obvious to me that I was not tapping in to the ability of every child and there was enthusiasm there to be found if only I could discover the way to release it.

I can now see that starting with the personal is probably the best and most natural place to start. I now believe that unless I understand myself as a learner then I can't make that leap forward to understand how the children I teach learn. So where am I now? Developing my own creative and philosophical thinking to research my question, 'How can I make the children more involved in their own learning?'

Joy's Account

It's simple, I love teaching. I am still excited by the children I teach, their way of thinking and expressing themselves and the possibilities of finding new unknown places to explore with them. I have a passion for learning and finding opportunities to experiment with new ideas, so I have come to challenge myself over the years to research my own learning and practice. I am now keen to take a risk and share the journey and learning with the wonderful and curious children I teach, and inspire them to be self-reflective learners.

My reflections and the initial forming of my educational values began with my youngest daughter, who is now 18, and clarifies where my journey of reflection started. Abi was born with problems in both ears and until she was 4 and a half had very little hearing. She had taught herself to lip read and after an operation, speech therapy began. Sounds around her terrified her and it was a slow process. My eldest daughter had learned to talk like all other children, by listening to speech around them. Abi had none of these experiences to draw upon and so the process of teaching her to talk was very different. We played lots of games, making the process very engaging and fun to maintain her concentration. The first seed of thought about wanting to teach and the teacher I wanted to be were planted. The time that I spent with Abi inspired me, fascinated me and began my journey.

A Shock to My System

At university I was shocked but fascinated at the way I was 'taught' to teach. The literacy hour was coming in at the time I started my first post and I remember being given a laminated clock from the strategy folder showing the necessary timings. I was monitored to make sure I was sticking to it exactly. At the end of each half term I was expected to calculate the percentage of time for each subject and hand this in to the senior management team; my life felt regimented, my dreams stifled! It felt very restrictive, as if we were caught in the past and afraid to say there were problems and try and solve them. Michael Bassey (1991) described my problem when he wrote, 'A second way of creating education is the historic way. It entails repeating what has been done before: basing today's action on the way it was done last week or last year. Again I guess that most of us work this way quite often, arguing that there is no time to do otherwise.'

It is reassuring I am not alone.

When I started I was teaching Year 1 children and my classroom could have been for Year 6 in that there was no provision for play. But as a newly qualified teacher I had no influence to change what the government was presenting us with. I am not sure how I wanted it to change. I just felt there should be so much more. The school had an Ofsted inspection during the year and we came out with a glowing report, so I had even less opportunity to influence any change. I had ideas but needed experience and the opportunities to experiment.

Changing schools brought a different experience of management and curriculum, which was exciting but still not what I had dreamt of. Being the Special Needs Co-ordinator and then deputy head gave me the opportunity to influence school policy and enthuse those around me. I was fortunate to be part of a team that was excited by change and willing to listen to ideas and debate them and, if they felt the ideas proven, would introduce them and later review with an open mind.

'Excellence and Enjoyment' Arrives

For me the journey of change and hope really began with the arrival of 'Excellence and Enjoyment' in 2003. For the first time I felt we had the opportunity to take the curriculum and review it with flexibility and enthusiasm. I remember reading the introduction by Charles Clarke (then Secretary of State for Education) twice, just to make sure I had understood the meaning correctly. 'There will be different ways. Children learn better when they are excited and engaged... different schools go about this in different ways. There will be sparks that make learning vivid and real for different children.'

For the first time since the rigidity of the Literacy and Numeracy Hours were introduced I felt able to really make changes that would matter and have an impact. We were explicitly being encouraged to develop creativity and flexible ways of thinking and learning. It was the door opening, full of opportunities for all of us to interpret and react to in our own way, if we had the vision and the courage!

Acting and Reflecting and Doing Things Differently

For the first time I felt a stirring of old memories, of the teacher I had wanted to be, before I was taught 'better'! This began my first cycle of action and reflecting on my values and how these could be interpreted into actions in my classroom.

One of the difficulties facing schools is the conflict between knowing that we want to change and the pressure to be seen to be maintaining levels of value added attainment. How do we balance the risk of change, with not changing and playing it safe, but being criticised for that too?

Many schools identify one area that they think they can introduce safely. Looking around, I was excited by the many possibilities and wanted so much more for my children and myself.

Many issues had rumbled around the staffroom and this gave me the incentive and opportunity to tackle them. The process of reflection identified small areas that my colleagues and I were unhappy with and provided small steps to take, before finding our way further.

We began developing RE, 'guided fantasies' and 'Circle Time', building the attitudes, values and skills of the whole child. It was quite daunting knowing where to begin, but the growing awareness of approaches such as Thinking Actively in a Social Context (TASC) developed by Belle Wallace, and 'Building Learning Power' developed by Guy Claxton, all came at the right time for me.

Reviewing the curriculum and assessment policy became my focus as I attended training sessions, visited other schools and developed my own professional development programme. My belief and enthusiasm that we could really achieve a manageable, exciting curriculum with more involved learners kept the midnight oil burning! The more I introduced into the classroom, the more I wanted to challenge and change my ideas and thinking. The Swiss philosopher, Henri Amiel, who lived in the 1800's, wrote, 'It is by teaching that we teach ourselves.' I found this quote a while ago and wrote it in my diary. Occasionally I catch a glimpse of it. I haven't kept it for any particular reason other than it strikes a chord in me and seems to link my thoughts together at the core.

I have found that new ideas I introduce are exciting and begin a new unseen path. A new idea often leads in a direction I hadn't anticipated, generating new challenges and chaotic notes. The Curriculum Map is an example. It had a huge impact, leading us to change the timetable, learn to be flexible and 'challenge our own thinking'.

The main worry for the staff was that we would come up with so many good ideas that it would be difficult to know which to adopt. We have all been in the situation where we have been inspired on a course, but with the best of intentions, when back in school, found it difficult to keep working on an idea before something else seems to come along, like Christmas, reports or children! I made sure we took a breath, planned carefully the way forward and what we wanted to include and prioritise in our school improvement plan, linking it all into a clear, concise vision that was manageable.

Getting Personalised

The next pivotal point came with the focus on personalised learning, which I knew I wanted to explore in a creative and stimulating learning environment. I wanted the children to understand what a good learner is like, the skills involved and that there is progression within those skills. I also wanted them to learn to understand themselves, the things that make them tick, their worries and strengths, the quirks that make them an individual and influence their emotional learning, the learner they are and the learner they could be. I believe it is in that way children begin to form their own values and articulate them to others. Costa & Kallick (2000) highlight this when they say, 'All human beings have the capacity to generate novel, clever or ingenious products, solutions, and techniques – if that capacity is developed.'

I wanted the children to have the opportunities to work creatively on any task with the freedom to think outside the box. I wanted them to be willing to take risks, to see learning as being flexible and fluid requiring different skills and responses and to think beyond their immediate learning and begin to generalise and create their own theories of learning.

Personalising learning enables a child to react to any learning situation with an understanding of self and the ability to empathise and evaluate, working with the learning skills of others around them. But this has to be in the context of a learning environment and a creative curriculum where the children are involved in developing their own educational theories. I wanted to develop a format for the children to explore learning, including theories of others, and use this as a platform to create their own knowledge and values, reviewing over time the narrative of their developing thinking.

Will a child in the future look back on school and value the 'pace and challenge' they constantly experienced in all 'good' lessons? I worry whether children have time to rest, to experience, to reflect or to explore learning as a skill. Will they only take away the knowledge context of lessons or have the skills to articulate their own learning experiences in a reflective, emotional responsive way, talking about the moments that were significant to them and the impact that has had on them? Will they have the vision to see forward or be caught in the cycle of maintaining the well-trodden path because we know it is successful? How do we know it is successful?

I wanted this to be part of a whole picture and not a one-off initiative that felt safe. Often we feel overloaded with new strategies even though we can see the benefit of them as they rush towards us. I wanted more. The whole package, ideas but also practical ways to introduce them into my classroom and across our school. I want this now, not in several years' time when things may come together. I did not want to keep exploring new ideas and finding out the hard way which ones are more successful than others. But I couldn't find a package which delivered or guided my thinking in the way I wanted to explore and felt my children deserved. The answer for me was to do it myself, plough through all that I had read and experienced, explore different paths, trial aspects with my class, then share what I had found with others.

Children as Action Researchers, with Me, Creating our Own Answers

I became familiar with TASC when all the local schools worked together on an area wide project. I continued to evolve my use of TASC after the project and subsequently focused on this work when I joined a group of teachers working on a Master's programme tutored by Jack Whitehead at the University of Bath. Jack introduced me to a Living Theory approach to action research. Living Theory is distinguishable by having, "'I' as a living contradiction, the use of action reflection cycles, the use of procedures of personal and social validation and the inclusion of a life-affirming energy with values as explanatory principles of educational influence.' (Whitehead and McNiff, 2006) This is explained more in Chapter 10.

One morning, following a session at the university with the Masters group, I talked about the research I was carrying out about learning with my class. The children were surprised and challenged me immediately; if I was writing about learning, didn't I need their help! The tone of their comment made me realise that they couldn't even comprehend that I could write about learning without help from the children.

It made me take a step back and look at learning in my classroom from a different perspective. Their ideas were thought provoking, challenged my thinking and helped me to begin to see as a learner through their eyes. This for me was an important step, to openly share with my class how I was feeling and that I wanted to explore ideas with them. The children and I became learners together, action researchers researching learners and learning. It is scary, moving from being the expert handing out knowledge, to becoming an equal learning partner, but I recommend you try it. The value you will both gain from the change in relationships and expectations will surprise you. I found my pupils to be exciting companions as they looked at the world through very different eyes.

We talked about what we believed about learning and how we learn. The perceptions and understandings of the children were fascinating. I discovered the work of Carol Dweck (2000) on fixed and growth mindsets as descriptions of how we perceive intelligence and the effect this has on our ability to approach learning opportunities. I shared this with the children and we talked it over.

Tina said that she thought we all have little factories in our brain with little people that work in them and store all the things we learn for us. It transpired that her mum had bought her a series of books called My Body that came out monthly for children to collect. It described the workings of the brain in pictures showing little people storing the information and Tina had just taken it literally. Tom started thinking about why we forget things when we have learned them. He spoke in a tone that implied the answer was obvious, we all keep things we have learned in a special wardrobe in our brain, sometimes if we forget where it is stored we cannot find it and use the memory. Whereas Ben described having little people that stored it safely for him in his head, but sometimes things leak and run down his neck, through his body and down his legs, out of his feet and into the ground. That is how he said he forgets things, because they have 'run' away.

This discussion started our thoughts about learning and what we would like to find out or explore together.

For the children to draw their memory was quite a challenge and resulted in some lovely pictures that we discussed and annotated together. We decided, and it was the children's idea, that we would make a floor book together with pockets to store film discs or extras and what we wrote about our thoughts and ideas.

We explored ourselves and our learning together, apart and in groups, where our perspectives, beliefs and values were challenged, probed and questioned. We changed. We all changed. We gained a greater understanding of what makes us 'tick', how we learn best, what impacts positively and negatively on our learning, but perhaps most importantly of all, we all developed a sense of educational responsibility towards the world and ourselves we interact with. But for all the understanding we created, Pat, who was only just seven years old, summed it up precisely when she said, 'The more I know, the more I know there is that I don't know.'

As our journey and understanding of ourselves deepened, the children's focus and concern moved from the centrality of themselves to worrying about other children and other schools and the opportunities they had to explore the benefits of understanding through research of learning.

This new way of learning and being learners together has evoked questions that I have no answer to. We explore big philosophical questions often to do with the meaning of life and our spiritual self that sometimes have no answers. But for the questions we have generated there should be answers, answers to be debated and thought about, but still answers:

- 'Why is it that only grown-ups write about learning?'
- 'Why don't grown-ups ask us about learning?'
- 'We are great learners, better than older people sometimes, but why don't they listen to us?'
- 'Can we change things in school?'

These are the topics that I have explored and talked about with my children. Often they have become an issue as the children have gained in confidence, developed their own sense of 'educational responsibility' and have begun to question the perceived and sometimes clear boundaries they feel are in place in school.

I have been trained to be a good teacher, to challenge all the children in my care, to monitor and track carefully and enable as many of my class as possible to reach 'Level 3' at the end of Key Stage 1. Ofsted judged my teaching as good and excellent and I fit the system and methods for teaching at the present time. However I have learned to bend and flex the system to the responsibility I feel towards my children and the ethos I treasure in my class.

SATs as an Opportunity?!

Our belief in ourselves as learners enables us to access and appreciate the different methods of teaching and learning we experience. The children made this very plain when we were discussing SATs just after they had finished. They were taken under exam conditions and I wondered how the children had felt. They were very clear and positive about the whole experience and enjoyed doing them. Every child! They talked about all of the different ways we learn, making me think of a jigsaw puzzle. This is just one piece, one experience that compliments and jars against others, but is a positive experience if we treasure all learning. The world the children will experience will not always be easy and will challenge them. This is how they made me feel listening to them and made me think about the skills they would need to access and take the positive from their learning experiences. I think Pat was right when she said, 'The more I know, the more I know there is that I don't know.'

I have fond memories of our journey and can, with hindsight, recognise the steps I was enabled to take and the opening up of opportunities, although I didn't see that at the time as I was caught up in the moment. I have found that value and learning comes from the moment, but also in reflecting back.

The skills and understandings developed through the TASC Wheel and exploring themselves and their learning gave the children creative and philosophical thinking skills with which to explore, in a greater way, the world around them, to challenge, question and see beneath the surface layer we often take at face value. It has given them the understanding that they can create knowledge and understanding from the collection of their learning, and that a space for learning can be controlled, developed and used by them. This is a range of new voices, with a keen and different perspective on learning, voices with a powerful message they are keen to share with both adults and other children.

Future Plans

I have recently become a headteacher of a primary school in Somerset. This has not only changed but also extended my awareness of the 'purpose' for creative and philosophical thinking. Over the next year, two of our INSET days will be based around developing 'learning' in our school and thinking about our vision for the future. The basis of action research through the format of the TASC Wheel will be introduced and used as a tool for staff development to enhance our learning as we introduce it to the children as well. The journey for our school will be shared, reflected on from different perspectives and linked together. Each member of staff will have an A4 ring binder for handouts, their thoughts in the form of notes, photos, pictures, video and reflections as a diary to inform their planning to introduce elements to the children. I am looking forward to sharing this learning log with the staff and children. Work, notes of discussions, philosophical questions, sticky notes of comments, printouts from interactive whiteboards and photographs will all add to a floor-book. By encouraging staff to develop a shared floor-book, as an evolving record of the journey within the class, I hope to learn how this helps to promote personal reflection on activity as well as enabling thinking to be shared and enhanced with others.

The time is now, break free and fly... if you have the courage!

Marie's Account

I don't know where my story begins, perhaps in my childhood with a tradition of question and argument and creative responses to problems. By argument I don't mean quarrel, but rather where a line of reasoning is formed, tested, revised and developed. Although maybe on reflection I am quarrelsome as well. I find it hard to just do what I am told, 'Why?' seems to spring from my lips almost before I am conscious of uttering the word.

Not because I wouldn't do whatever it is but because I assume there must be a reason which I haven't understood. If someone makes a universal claim of, 'This is the way it is,' or, 'This is the way it must be done,' I find myself thinking, and on occasions saying, 'Is that right?' and 'How are you so sure about that?' and 'What if…?'

I have always found people fascinating and questions just bubble up: 'Why did they do that?'; 'Why did they change?'; 'How did they come to think that?' Questions and people – no wonder psychology has kept me fascinated for nearly four decades. No right questions, no universal right answers, just the most fantastic stories of lives as learning journeys, each unique with their own distinct, ever evolving commentaries and explanations.

And So to School

After dipping my toe into psychology as an undergraduate student I trained as a teacher. This was in those heady days before the National Curriculum, targets and Ofsted. A large part of my year teaching ten year olds was spent trying to work out what I should fill the days with. Maths was sorted. I had the bottom set and I was given details of what the children had to learn. My challenge was how to enable them to understand it enough to remember it and be interested enough to avoid mayhem breaking out. Dean had a particular way of letting me know when I had got it wrong, which spurred me to become increasingly creative in my thinking.

Having little knowledge of anything to impart of history, geography or other subjects I wondered what I would find interesting and why. I involved the children in my problem and creating a solution that would bring them to these subjects with interest and enthusiasm. In geography we learned to ask together, 'What questions would be interesting to ask about a country?' and shared our thinking on how they might go about answering their questions. They worked in pairs and small groups for the most part to choose a country and each had a section of the classroom wall to display their discoveries. We spent hours writing to embassies, collecting travel brochures, inspecting tin labels for country of origin, searching through the stock cupboard for long forgotten books. One child I remember chose Scotland for her inquiry. I tried to persuade her that Scotland was not appropriate as it was not a foreign country. She won the argument and did a lovely piece of work. This was before devolution was dreamt of, but her thinking was obviously ahead of her time or had a crystal ball.

History was sorted by each group choosing a century and creating questions that interested them, such as, 'If I lived then what would I have for breakfast?', 'How would I keep warm?', 'What would I have to play with?', 'Would I be able to play or would I have to do something else?' Having no Internet and a pretty limited variety of books we ended up with more about who was on the throne at the time than answers to the questions we had, which posed other interesting questions, like 'Why are most history books about Kings?' One child found different accounts of the same event in a couple of books and that set them off trying to check consistency and to ask whether facts were facts and how we could be sure.

Looking back I can appreciate now how much I learned about creative and philosophical thinking from those ten year olds. My year in a remedial department and unit for disturbing pupils in a secondary school taught me that education is about teaching people not subjects. Teaching young people to read and write is as much about enabling them to believe they can learn and want to as it is about enabling them to acquire skills. I am not sure how much my pupils learned that year but it was a major educational experience for me. I was constantly faced with philosophical questions like, 'What is the purpose of school?', 'What is the relevance of what I am teaching to the lives of Harry, Marlene, Danny…?' Creative thinking became not a luxury but an essential survival tool, especially for Friday afternoons.

And Moving Swiftly On…

Fast forwarding through 20 odd years as a school psychologist I began to explore 'high ability' in the mid 90's. My interest and project grew to the point that I moved out of the school psychology service to work fulltime as a senior educational psychologist, developing and co-ordinating an inclusive gifted and talented education project for the local authority.

I began to wonder, 'How do you know what you want to do if you don't know what it is?' It seemed to be that at some point people found their dream when they noticed parents, relations or friends of the family doing what inspired them, or there was a happy accidental meeting with a person or idea that ignited a spark. I wanted to expand the opportunity for children to have that happy accident so I began to organise workshops for children and young people on Saturdays, provided by experts who could communicate their passion in the field. Ten years on and they are still running.

The children vote with their feet and many have continued to apply for places. If I feel I am loosing touch with what I am doing and why, I go along to a workshop. The enthusiasm of the children and adults always cheers me up and revitalises me. What are they about? I summarised it at the start of a paper I titled, The Elasticated Learner: Beyond Curriculum Learning Opportunities in a Local Education Authority:

> 'After one Saturday workshop, Chris, an 11 year old, told me he was becoming an 'elasticated learner'. This seems to succinctly sum up the purpose of education in general and the Able Pupils Extending Opportunities (APEX) out of hours sessions in particular, with the emphasis being not only on flexible, increased capacity but also on the ownership by the learner of the process. How can we help more young people to become 'elasticated learners'; high ability learners willing and able to seek out and profit from learning experiences which will challenge and extend them, take them to new and uncharted territory and contribute to their educational voyage?' (Huxtable, 2003)

The workshops are intended to give children an opportunity to meet and work with others with similar interests and abilities, work with expert role-models, increase their understanding of the variety of possible areas to explore, have fun and feel a sense of accomplishment, and develop some skills.

Over the years we have run workshops on juggling, maths magic, Chinese brush painting, poetry, a trial of Jack from *Jack and the Beanstalk*… the list is endless. A common and recurring response from children and adults is, 'They are not like school!' Workshop providers who are teachers tell me that it is the best in-service training. They engage in their own thinking, their own passion for learning, and that is communicated to the children.

I am very clear that the purpose is not merely to transmit information or skills, but rather for children and adults to engage actively in thinking and creating new knowledge which contributes to the process of learning. As a consequence what each person learns is different and personal to them. One child may learn that they can overcome their fear of going somewhere new, another may learn a new technique for holding a brush, another that engineers use creative thinking skills… and occasionally one may find a small spark that later contributes to the fire of their vocation.

As I developed the project I began clarifying to myself what I was doing and why. It began to emerge that what I was doing was making a contribution that would enable the children to develop their own aspirations. Through providing the opportunities in the workshops I was setting up situations to help them pursue their interests with confidence and competence, where they would not only benefit as individuals, but would also share their learning with others.

Thinking About It

I started exploring what it meant to be a 'high ability' learner. Not surprisingly I rapidly came to the conclusion that the terms 'high ability learning' and 'higher order thinking' were often used almost interchangeably, particularly when it came to the practical issues concerning what to do in the classroom.

Benjamin Bloom returned to my life and it was running a workshop on Bloom that I first met Ros. 'Bloom's Taxonomy' (Bloom, 1956) is still a favourite in training material on thinking, questioning and learning. I found it worth getting hold of a copy of the original book rather than the often simplistic and limited representations offered at some training courses.

There's nothing like the challenge of running a workshop to force me to get my thoughts in some sort of order, extend my reading and develop my thinking. Through doing that I discovered Robert Fisher. His description of philosophy for children as thinking about thinking, and a creative process of inquiry made sense to me and I found his distinction between different forms of thinking useful.

Elements of Thinking Based on Robert Fisher's Work

Everyday thinking	Critical thinking
Guessing	Estimating
Preferring	Evaluating
Assuming	Justifying
Associating/listing	Classifying
Accepting	Hypothesising
Judging	Analysing
Inferring	Reasoning

I organised days for teachers locally with national speakers that I found stimulating and asked Robert to do a session. The interest was so high I asked him back on a number of occasions. His books such as Stories for Thinking and Poems for Thinking continue to be popular resources for many of the teachers I work with.

My understanding of what I was doing and why began to extend. I wanted to enhance the opportunities for children to grow as thoughtful learners – learners with lots of ideas – able to reflect and make reasoned and reasonable decisions, with a growing knowledge of themselves.

And so I developed my notions of inclusive gifted and talented education. I understand gifts and talents not as the defining categories of traditional theory and practice but as living educational concepts; dynamic, evolving, inter-relational and based on values. Daisaku Ikeda (2004), president of an international Buddhist association, expresses something of this kind in this extract:

> 'Being talented does not mean just being a good musician, writer or athlete. There are many kinds of talent. You may be a great conversationalist, or make friends easily, or be able to put others at ease… Without doubt, you possess your special jewel, your own unique talent. In the same way, each of us has a mission that only we can fulfil. That mission will not be found somewhere far away, in doing something special or extraordinary. Even those people who seem to have led great lives have really only done what they felt they had to do in order to truly be themselves. We realise our purpose in life by doing our very best where we are right at this moment, by thinking about what we can do to improve the lives of those right around us.'

I went to a session that Belle Wallace ran at a National Association of Able Children in Education (NACE) conference on TASC and subsequently asked her to run sessions for me in the authority. I have had the delight of getting to know Belle and her work over the years. It offers an elegant, content free frame for children and adults developing their inquiries and research. Why have I come more and more to see research as important for children and educators to be engaged in? I think Elliot Eisner (1993) said it really well, '…we do research to understand. We try to understand in order to make our schools better places for both the children and the adults who share their lives there.'

It was working with teachers to develop their understandings of TASC (Wallace et al, 2004) and its use in their practice that I first met Joy. You will find a lot more about TASC in this book, particularly in Chapters 8, 9 and 10.

The more I looked into 'thinking' the more material and writers I found. I know that one lifetime is simply not long enough to get to grips with all of it and I thought, 'How do I make a decision as to what to use?' Staffroom tables were beginning to groan under the weight of the latest 'Thinking' offering, the latest quick fix packages and training by charismatic gurus, tips for this and tips for that. How was a teacher to make sense of it all in a busy classroom with the curriculum to deliver?

I had been using Jo Renzulli's (1985) ideas to inform my work plan and found it useful for teachers to decide what they wanted to 'do' about 'thinking'. He has a notion of three types of learning opportunities.

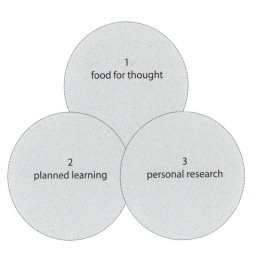

Type 1 – The 'one-offs', the sort of 'thinking' activity that might be squeezed in at the odd moment, like brainstorming 101 ways of using a pop bottle, the one-off activities like inventing a travel buggy for a Martian, the learning opportunities that:

- provide food for thought
- give a taste
- open eyes, broaden horizons, take you to the unknown
- illustrate 'thinking' in other disciplines, domains, areas of endeavour
- arouse curiosity
- offer surprises, challenges
- allow playfulness and experimentation with ideas.

Type 2 – This is where we might teach how to carry out an inquiry through TASC or run Philosophy for Children sessions so the children learn Socratic questioning and participating in a community of inquiry.

This is the learning with planned learning outcomes, which provide opportunities to acquire information, learn the skills and strategies:

- needed to perform as an expert
- which enable you to learn how to learn and think efficiently and effectively
- to study effectively and efficiently
- to collaborate with others
- to manage a project/inquiry.

Type 3 – The opportunity to be a knowledge-creating researcher, where you behave as an expert thinker. This is the time where children can focus on something that they are really interested in and use their research skills to create new knowledge about the world and about themselves, use TASC in practice to create a disciplined inquiry. This is where they can focus on creating their own living theory account and come to know themselves, their values, their passions and the lives they want to lead which they would find satisfying and productive. These are opportunities to pursue those areas of personal interest to you in more depth, to explore, to experiment, to boldly go where you have not been before, opportunities to develop a passion for learning. An opportunity to behave as an expert:

- to inquire into an area of personal interest
- in a disciplined manner
- with a valued outcome
- within a time frame.

The three types of learning opportunities are not necessarily pursued systematically from 1 to 2 to 3; instead they have a more dynamic inter-relationship. For instance the outcome of a type 3 opportunity (a personal in-depth inquiry) could provide a type 1 (a taster) for someone else, and could lead the learner to seek specific skills through a type 2 opportunity.

The Saturday workshops provide tasters, type 1. At one workshop two ten year olds learned Chinese brush painting. When they went back to school they developed and ran a workshop for other children. They engaged in a type 3 sort of activity. There they taught the other children particular techniques, they offered a type 2 opportunity for the other children. At another workshop on the body a young child became so excited he went back to school and continued to find out all he could about the body and began to ask questions he hadn't thought about before and find out what was already known, He was beginning to develop his inquiry which might become a type 3 activity, researching as an expert.

I have found that this sort of approach to making decisions about 'thinking' at least enables me to make reasoned and reasonable decisions about what to do and it has made sense to the teachers I have introduced it to.

The most recent influence on my thinking has been through finding the work of Jack Whitehead (www.actionresearch.net). His idea of a Living Theory, which is the explanation, I give for the educational influence I have in my own learning, that of others and in social organisations, such as schools, provided the last part of my puzzle. I began to really appreciate the knowledge we all bring to what we do and the theories we have which we often are not aware of but which are fundamental influences in the way we live our lives. I came to ask again, 'Why do I do what I do?' My answer was that I wanted children to grow as people who are comfortable in their own skin, knowing themselves, liking themselves, at peace with themselves, knowing what they want to work on, to improve, and to have the courage to change and accept their own stumbling and that of other people as part of the journey.

I believe that individuals learn what they see themselves capable of learning and what is of value to them. The striving for excellence seems to carry with it a hope of personal fulfilment and when that personal ambition coincides with the needs of others, it carries with it a hope for the progression of all of us and 'twice affirmation' for the individual.

I work from the premise that all children and young people hold within themselves the possibility of living a satisfying and productive life and the ability to make a valued and valuable contribution to their own life and the life of us all. I believe there is no predetermined limit as to what that contribution might be. I do not mean that I believe a child is able to grow up to achieve anything they might choose, rather I believe it is not possible to predict what they might achieve during their lifetime through the combination of opportunity and their determined inclination and commitment to realising their aspirations. My purpose as an educator is to open the imaginations of children and young people to the various possibilities of living satisfying and productive lives so they can make informed decisions as to what they want to do as they enter the adult world.

I believe the individual is the only one who can determine whether their life is satisfying and productive, and they do so according to their own living values as standards by which to make such judgments.

And that is where I am now – trying to walk my own talk and learn from trying to understand and improve my own theories to explain what I do, contributing to improving the educational experience of children and young people.

The Progression of our Thinking and Where Next

All our stories have a linking thread despite the differences between the age groups and experiences. We have each come, in our own way, to value creative and philosophical thinking in our work as educators, valuing the children as individuals with important ideas and thoughts about the educational provision they want and can respond to, and the educational influence they can have in their own lives. We have moved forward into creating situations and opportunities where their views and abilities are used to guide their learning. Our job is not so much to fill them to the brim with accepted knowledge, but to enable them to be partners in the creation of their own knowledge and work with others to create new, meaningful knowledge.

Part 2

Developing Children's Thinking with a Purpose

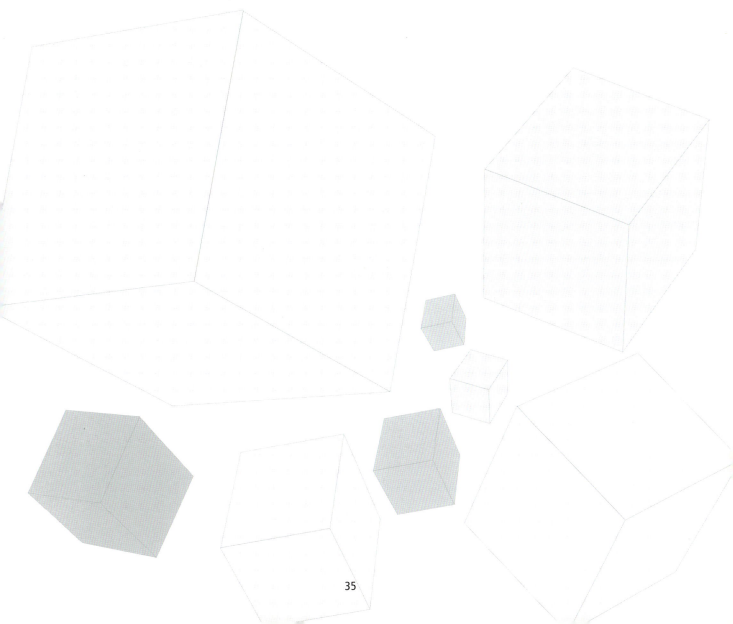

Chapter 3

Encouraging Playful and Experimental Thinking Outside the Box

'It's never enough just to tell people about some new insight. Rather, you have to get them to experience it in a way that evokes its power and possibility. Instead of pouring knowledge into people's heads, you need to help them grind a new set of eyeglasses so they can see the world in a new way.'

John Seely Brown

'If at first the idea is not absurd, then there is no hope for it.'

Albert Einstein

'It is better to have enough ideas for some of them to be wrong, than to be always right by having no ideas at all.'

Edward De Bono

Why it is Important

Children as humans are born with a natural curiosity about the world and about themselves as places of creation. It seems strangely ironic that adults in business spend a fortune trying to get people to teach them to do what they were so good at before they went to school.

Opportunities to play with ideas, to experiment with ways of looking at the world and problems, to pursue the wisps of thoughts to where they might take you without the constraints of knowing where you are going, are key to continuing to develop attitudes, attributes, skills and understandings for the world of tomorrow. William Blake sums up why this is important when he said, 'What is now proved was once only imagined.' That is the basis of all progress. Tomorrow exists only in our imaginations. Death, in Terry Pratchet's Hogfather, commented on how imagination, curiosity and experimental thinking are at the basis of evolving values as a society.

> 'Take the universe and grind it down to the finest powder and sieve it through the finest sieve and then show me one atom of justice, one molecule of mercy, and yet,' Death waved his hand. 'And yet you act as if there is some ideal order in the world as if there is some... rightness in the universe by which it may be judged... You need to believe in things that aren't true. How else can they become?'

Sir Peter Medawar (1969), who won a Nobel prize for his work in the medico-biological field, expressed the connection poetically when he said, 'The utter non-sensicality of dreams – their glorious emancipation from the confinements of time and place and cause and sense – is probably the most significant thing about them, the property from which the student of mind has most to learn.'

We like this summing up by W. H. H. Gordon (2007), 'The ultimate solutions to problems are rational; the process of finding them is not.' So the ability to play and experiment with thinking is at the core of so many lifelong endeavours. Edward De Bono (2007) suggests that many intelligent people put a lot of energy into maintaining the status quo instead of using it to find more creative and interesting alternatives. We can speculate as to why; fear of the unknown, a personal investment in things remaining the same, relinquishing control, experience in school; the reasons are many. There are adults who seriously think that much of the world of imagination and creativity is just part of childhood and once we reach a certain level of maturity it should be left behind. We as educators feel this is a sad state of affairs that we can do something about. Through our development of creative and philosophical thinking activities in schools we are able to encourage future adults to keep that imaginative spark alive and hopefully rekindle it in the adults they work with. Too often the adult sees the cardboard box as just that and forgets the time when it could have been a spaceship or submarine. We forget that wonderfully exciting time when the world was to be explored, the unknown was not to be feared and endless questions came from our lips.

Using structures such as TASC we are also able to develop the way we present curriculum opportunities to the children so they are able to explore ideas, share their thoughts and guide their own learning. By giving them the green light on being able to experiment with thoughts and ideas without the constraints of a 'right' answer, we help them construct their own knowledge independently and with others.

Making Time and Making Links

Opportunities for putting in creative thinking or philosophy ideas can always be found in the timetable if you are determined and feel they are valuable. You can put a toe in the water rather than dive in at the deep end by finding the odd moments that can be freed up. Your pleasure should be a driving force in this. Determination might be the starting point, but a sense of enjoyment will enable you to continue and develop your own activities.

Ros looked at her early morning routines. She found 15 minutes at the start of the day, once a week, that she could set aside as time for creative thinking activities. Looking back she thinks it would have been far better to have chosen a time when she wasn't trying to do the register, count sandwich boxes and listen to snippets of news. It wasn't an ideal situation, but it was better than nothing. She wasn't sure how it was going to work or what the results would look like but she knew the type of response she wanted from the children. It's that 'buzz' of enthusiasm and excitement when you don't have to nag them to stay on task, when their faces are animated and they are reluctant to stop.

Getting Started

Ros began with several of Edward De Bono's ideas, which the children loved. For instance, designing a dog exercising machine (De Bono, 1970), or a special bed for people who have difficulty going to sleep (De Bono, 1972). She adapted ideas garnered from magazines, the Sunday newspapers, as well as books on creative thinking and came up with her own challenges such as:

- Invent gadgets to do your homework for you.
- Design transport for a land where wheels haven't been invented.

The more 'out of the box' the idea, the greater the enthusiasm of the children.

Robert Fisher (1995) has some great ideas too, such as, how many different ways can you change a circle, how many things can you get into a matchbox.

These types of activities don't require a lot of materials or preparation and can be continued in odd moments when children have finished some of their curriculum work. They are accessible to all children whatever their ability to write or articulate their thinking and can provide a welcome release for some children from the common demands of curricula tasks.

Thinking onto paper can take several forms and each child uses what suits her for a particular purpose. Children are gradually introduced to different techniques such as how to draw a simple mind map. Ros has found that while some are reluctant to use this format and prefer to write their ideas out in full, other children thrive when they become adept. She reminds them that she is interested in their response, and whether they have come up with original and creative ideas, not whether they are good at drawing, writing or mind mapping.

When you first start out it is difficult for teachers to remember that creative ideas don't necessarily come to order. Learning to be patient and not to fill the space with preconceived ideas as to what is creative and what is not is probably one of the hardest things for a teacher. We have found that it is not uncommon to find one or two children will just sit and appear to do nothing, sometimes for several sessions. This can happen for a number of reasons.

Sometimes the stimulus just isn't working for that child. Some of us think fast, others of us think much, much more slowly. Sometimes there are other things going on in the child's life that are consuming their attention. Sometimes a child needs to test the honesty of the space being given by doing nothing to see how you react. Sometimes the creative idea will turn up a couple of days later. As educators we have become used to results within a limited time scale, but rarely is this the case in 'real' life.

We have found the evaluation of the quality of education through high-stakes testing has cramped the creative thinking and damaged the confidence of many teachers. There is a relentless drive for pace and challenge, with lessons carefully planned to deliver on pre-declared learning outcomes, which leaves no space for day dreaming and exercising unfettered imagination. It can take time for both children and teacher to feel at ease to enjoy finding their own ideas, to feel confident with uncertainty and to experiment without knowing where they are going.

If you are feeling uncomfortable about this, try reminding yourself that there is no pressure. Ten or fifteen minutes doing a short activity is not a lot in the grand scheme of things. We have all experienced those lessons which don't quite fill the time allocated or the children's attention wanders. We've watched the rain fall at playtime or waited for the visitor who arrives late. There are always those little spaces in the school week when you may find yourself reaching for the quick time-filler activities. What we have tried to do, and the way we found helpful in gradually developing some of these activities, was to see them as 'time-fillers' but with the intention of tuning into natural curiosity and creativity, rather than just filling up time and keeping children busy.

When the child sees other children getting excited about what they are doing and ideas begin to flow round the class these sessions eventually become irresistible. Allowing a classroom assistant to join in is also helpful as it provides a good adult role model and you will find that adults also enjoy exercising their imaginations. This also includes you. Try joining in the session and practising what you preach. It will give you insights into what the children may be feeling and what might be needed to make the classroom culture one where creative thinking and diverse thinkers are valued. Children learn a lot from seeing what adults do, not just what they say. Seeing you enjoying experimenting and taking risks with your thinking can be inspirational for children to see, more so than what you actually create.

Another Step

After Ros had introduced the children to designing and inventing ideas, which they could do individually, she went on to try a more structured approach to helping them to learn how to evaluate some of their ideas. She used Edward De Bono's format of plus, minus and interesting thoughts to start with. This method encourages children to think of positive aspects of a situation, negative aspects and the ones that don't fit so neatly. These can be the ones that are the most interesting and invite further exploration. (This can also be very useful in staff meetings when trying to decide which idea to adopt but be warned, the 'interesting' column grows as you practise it.)

She moved on to use this approach to introduce the children to discussing imagined possibilities such as:

- What would happen if we travelled above ground on broomsticks?
- What would being invisible be like?

The children were put in small groups to discuss questions to start with so they could all have their turn to say something and be stimulated by hearing their classmates. At this point Ros was focusing on:

- encouraging the children to listen to one another and to give reasons for their opinions
- encouraging the children to think creatively
- developing their confidence to ask questions to which there might be no answer
- stimulating their curiosity about life.

The 15 minutes would start with Ros introducing the question or designs and reminding them to talk together about plus, minus and interesting. After the children had spent five minutes talking together they were invited to share their thinking with the class.

To begin with the children were inclined to listen only to their own ideas, but given time and help they learned to listen to each other. Initially Ros encouraged them to say why they agreed or disagreed with someone else's thinking. Eventually they began to respond to what was said by extending and building from the contributions to the discussion. More recently she has incorporated aspects of Assessment for Learning (AfL) in these feedback sessions by asking children to explain another child's thinking or tell the class of someone else's idea that they really liked. This helps the confidence of shy children and we all feel good when someone else reinforces one of our ideas.

Their ideas were endless. Sometimes Ros would think of the topic and at other times the children themselves came up with something they wanted the class to investigate or consider. For instance, the children considered:

- what an ideal world would be like and whether everyone would have a similar core criteria (personally I can live without computer games and hamburgers but I had to accept I was in a minority – a good thing to learn)
- what their parents had worried about at their age
- what would the effect be of 24 hour shopping
- whether schools should be abolished.

The usual role for the teacher is to lead or direct or dispense knowledge. These activities require a different role and it can take time for both the teacher and the children to get used to it. Once you have had some experience of using sessions like this you might find it useful to set up a video camera in the corner of the classroom and play it back so you can see whether you are facilitating, rather than leading the thinking. Initially though, make your intention one of feeling comfortable with what you are doing, gaining pleasure and insight from it. Introducing non-judgemental responses, such as 'thank you', rather than 'great idea!' and holding the silence while the children think are techniques you can develop gradually and review through the use of video.

Using these techniques, Ros found some of the questions and responses went deeper than she had anticipated. For instance, abolishing school got a 'thumbs up' from most of the children to start with. Not surprisingly they said it would be great because they would be able to play more and do less work. Ros encouraged them to give more pros and cons, pushing them to think outside the box. They began to ask questions. If they were not in school who would look after them? Would their mum have to give up work? If she did who would give them pocket money?

It can be hard not to close the thinking down. For instance, when Jamey said it didn't matter because he could look after himself, Ros knew his circumstances and was able to thank him for his contribution and ask for other thoughts. She resisted the adult's inclination to give chapter and verse as to why this is not allowed and trusted in the children to bring these out. The children very soon realised that hanging around just playing all day was a bit limited, caused problems for parents and left you pretty short on literacy and numeracy skills if you ever wanted to earn a living. Given a space to work through their thoughts they began to see that sometimes the cons outweighed the pros and that the first ideas were not always the best. We have found that it takes time to learn how to probe that little bit more and expect a deeper response from the children.

To give you more of a taste of how a session went Ros describes a little of what happened when she posed the question, 'What would be the effect of all animal life disappearing from the planet?' This time the topic lasted two sessions.

The children started by listing all the things we wouldn't have such as McDonalds and leather shoes, absence of pets, farmers without livestock and so on. Then someone questioned whether that meant humans wouldn't be there either as they are animals, not plants.

By the end of the second session the general consensus was that the planet could well be in a mess and there were far more questions as a result; would grass continue to grow if there were no animals to eat it, would certain plants like weeds push out other plants, would lakes and rivers clog up with weed, would the plant species adapt and evolve?

In terms of having something 'chewy' to discuss, it was fabulous. The classroom was animated and buzzing – and that's still a sensation that gives her intense pleasure, because it means that the children are not passive participants in the learning activities, but are stamping their own identities on the discussion and developing their own muscle as learners. Moreover, Ros is involved in doing what she feels to be the essential value of her job; not filling them with a mass of information, but encouraging them to be independent learners with an open curiosity.

I believe if we encourage children to take time out from 'real life' to think in this way, then we are preserving some of that creativity for them to enjoy in later life.

Where to Next?

At the start of a new school year Ros gives each child an unlined jotter or 'Thinking Book' in which they can draw, map out or jot down their ideas. These are not marked for neatness, spelling or against a learning objective as the overall purpose is to help the children reflect, create and organise their thoughts in a way that suits them. She reminds the children that the book is for them to map out their ideas – scribble notes, diagrams, odd words or pictures and they can use them to make a quick note of something they want to do when they have the time or opportunity.

Joy gives the children plain white A5 ring binders with a cover into which you can slip paper. She encourages her children to personalise the covers in whatever way they choose so they develop a sense of ownership. This has become a fun and creative activity with imaginations let off the leash. Some have slipped in drawings; others have embellished the sheet with a variety of materials including feathers, string patterns and spirals of crinkle cut paper. Every so often the children design new covers which reflect their thinking at the time. This refreshes the books and encourages the children to look back over their previous ideas and reappraise them. The children wanted to keep photos and mementos to remind them of thoughts they want to return to. They made pockets to stick inside the covers to hold them. By giving the children control over what they share Joy reduces the children's inhibitions to be creative by allowing privacy.

The children are encouraged to experiment and create different ways of representing their thinking; pictures, models, diagrams, maps, ciphers, words. Some people find it easier to put ideas into pictures and find using words to describe concepts difficult and visa versa.

Ros found her preferred way of working was to translate her ideas into diagrams or pictures. Being able to represent mathematical concepts in visual form brought her lots of genuine 'eureka' moments and transferred her understanding to a deeper level. Obviously this will not suit everyone, but the important thing to remember is that we all have different preferred ways of learning. If we want to encourage children to maximise their learning and understanding we need to accept this may not always be represented in neat handwritten form with correct punctuation and spelling or grammatically correct utterances. Guy Claxton (2001) shows some of the consequences when he quotes the results of Robert Sternberg's research, who asserted that, 'Students with creative and practical abilities are essentially "iced out" of the system, because at no point are they allowed to let their abilities shine through and help them perform better... the result is that career paths may be barred to intellectually talented individuals.'

Chapter 4

Developing the Ability of Children to Pose Questions that are Important to them and Create Answers

'You can tell whether a man is clever by his answers. You can tell whether a man is wise by his questions.'

Naguib Mahfouz

Why it is Important

It is generally forgotten that our current curriculum is comprised of answers or responses to questions that people considered important at some point in the past. The reasons for them asking these questions or needing to find an answer have disappeared into the mists of time along with the research stories or narratives that link answer to question. This was made very real for Marie at a Saturday workshop she had organised for young people run by Professor Chris Budd at the University of Bath.

Chris is a passionate mathematician in love with his subject. He usually begins his workshops by giving the historical context of whatever is the subject of the session. This session on quadratic equations was no exception. He started his workshop by asking, 'Who invented quadratic equations?' and then, 'Why did they invent them?' It had never occurred to Marie before that there were real people wrestling with real problems whose persistent struggle to improve their response generated 'quadratic equations' as an answer to their question. She could visualise some poor Babylonian farmer faced with the problems of how many fields to plant to keep his family fed and pay the king his taxes as Chris told the group about the evidence of this in the British Museum which had excited him. Memory, of course, is notoriously unreliable and the story of quadratic equations may well be wrong, but it was the living connection between an answer which sits in the curriculum and the question that gave it life that made the impression.

Chris has a way of exciting people about maths by helping them to look at the world with mathematicians' eyes. They feel his sense of excitement at creating questions that are important to him and his delight in finding the surprises that his efforts to create satisfying answers provide him with. During the workshop Chris went on to describe other problems that quadratic equations could help find an answer to. One problem concerned the trajectory of flying pigs. Various soft toys, pigs amongst them, soon filled the space of the lecture theatre as the young people got to work enthusiastically testing the theory themselves. By introducing creative thinking and questioning the young people became involved in something more real and exciting than just being shown how to use quadratic equations in a maths lesson, and many began to see how solving problems with mathematics is also a creative and imaginative experience. Mathew Lipman (2003) expresses this well when he describes 'education as inquiry' and explains:

'John Dewey was convinced that education had failed because it was guilty of a stupendous category mistake. It confused the refined, finished end products of inquiry with the raw, crude initial subject matter of inquiry and tried to get students to learn the solutions rather than investigate the problems and engage in inquiry for themselves. Just as scientists apply scientific method to the exploration of problematic situations so students should do the same if they are ever to learn to think for themselves. Instead, we ask them to study the end results of what the scientists have discovered; we neglect the process and fixate upon the product. When problems are not explored at first hand, no interest or motivation is engendered, and what we continue to call education is a charade and a mockery. Dewey had no doubt that what should be happening in the classroom is thinking – and independent, imaginative, resourceful thinking at that. The route he proposed

– and here some of his followers part company with him – is that the educational process in the classroom should take as its model the process of scientific inquiry.'

Making Time and Making Links

We work in a world of constraints. A lot of our time is spent teaching within the constraints of the instructions handed down to us from the Department of Children Schools and Families (DCSFs). However, although it is not always possible to have the degree of inquiry we would like, we can bring thinking about questions into our 'regular' curriculum work. As the children learn to recognise questions and create answers they are more able to actively engage in their curriculum work. Science is an easy place to recognise this process because it involves asking questions and finding answers, but look for opportunities to extend these questions, to rouse curiosity beyond the main 'scientific facts' that the curriculum demands. Knowing how an electrical circuit works and what the components are called is very useful within the system, but have you ever wondered, as one child did, what happens to the electricity when it has gone round the circuit and why were those colours chosen for the wires? An inquiring approach is also easily brought into other subjects. Why do we learn about Romans? Why don't we learn about Chinese or Indian history? What would it be like not to have zero? Does 1+1 always equal 2?

Getting Started

One of the simplest of ways to make a start on developing the children's creative and philosophical thinking is to focus on questions. Teachers already ask questions all day long. Sometimes these are very closed and practical, ensuring the children have understood what they are doing or what they need to use. Reflect back on a recent lesson and you will identify a wide range of questions. As we already use this form of teaching, it makes it an ideal place to start.

Using well-known fairy stories or fables is a very good way of moving the children into more creative questioning, largely because you can have such fun with the topics. Raising questions about Cinderella or Rapunzel may seem purely a diversion from 'real' life, but beneath the frivolous nature of the subjects lies the key to developing a very important ability, the ability to make a creative response to a new situation.

This links to the higher levels of questioning and intellectual activity outlined in Bloom's Taxonomy. To be able to raise questions about a frog prince or explore the implications of a change in history is to demonstrate an understanding beyond the obvious, a flexibility of interpretation and awareness that what you see in life depends on where you are standing at the time. It develops that ability encouraged by De Bono that we put our energies into creative responses to situations rather than into maintaining what has been before.

When children and adults are allowed to raise their own questions in a 'safe' situation they will not only find it a pleasant and enjoyable experience, but they will be developing their own creative thinking muscles which then can be applied to more serious subjects. They will also begin to appreciate the diversity to be found within groups of people, and value their own uniqueness as part of a greater collaboration of uniqueness. As Sternberg (1996) suggests:

'Creativity, then, is as much a matter of an attitude towards life as it is one of ability. Young children naturally display this kind of creativity. It is only in older children and adults that it is so hard to find, not because the potential is missing but because creativity has been suppressed by systems of raising and teaching children that encourage intellectual conformity.'

Each child was given a piece of scrap paper and pencil, and all were encouraged to jot down any thought that came to mind during the reading or telling of the story. They might have been street-wise Year 6 children, but they still enjoyed listening to Cinderella or Rumplestiltskin, and they particularly seemed to find it fun to unpick the story with questions:

- Why didn't Cinderella run away if she had a Fairy Godmother anyway to look after her?

- Why were her slippers made of glass – it's all hard and cold and would hurt your feet? We are still looking for a reasonable answer to that one.

- How come she had just the right things for the Fairy Godmother?

- Would you really marry someone because they fit a shoe?

These activities have worked just as well with other age groups. Any story that contains an element of fantasy will inspire questions. The children still listen to traditional stories purely for pleasure and entertainment and they can still be enjoyable when you give them a 'reality' check.

Once the children had written their questions they wrote them all on a flipchart so everyone had a chance to read their question out to the class and hear the questions that others were asking. The children were then asked to talk over the questions in small groups and to say which ones interested them and why. The exploration of questions is as much a part of the process of learning to appreciate the different qualities of a question as the more obvious stages of asking and answering. Some children found this quite difficult initially because school to them was about pleasing the adult with the correct answer. For others, who maybe didn't come up with that pleasing right answer too often, it was a relief to have their response valued in terms of originality rather than correctness.

The problem of which question they should select to explore in greater depth was resolved by giving each child three votes. With three votes the children could vote for their own question but they had still to think about other children's questions. The likelihood of a question getting no votes at all was significantly reduced, which the children took confidence from. There are strong links here with the structure for a Philosophy for Children (P4C) session, but an awareness of this work was to come later. Early activities were very much the result of professional intuition and trial and error.

The next task was to think of as many answers to those questions as possible. They were encouraged to be creative and not to dismiss anything out of hand. So, for example, when it came to why Cinderella needed glass slippers there were some interesting (and amusing) ideas:

- She'd just put pink nail varnish on her toes and she wanted everyone to see it.

- Glass is waterproof and it was raining outside.

- They'd last longer.

- She wanted to be different.

- You can wear glass with any colour.

At this early stage there was not a great deal of discussion about the feasibility of the answers. The emphasis was on encouraging the children to hear their own voices, listen to others and gain the confidence to talk. What was very obvious in these sessions was that they were great fun. Once the children realised that a standard 'right' answer was not expected, they allowed themselves to stretch their imaginations and think extremely creatively. It wasn't only the children who found the sessions fun, either. Not only did creating imaginative answers suit Ros's sense of humour but other adults working in the classroom would get quite carried away. On one memorable occasion the story under discussion was Rumplestiltskin. One of the questions that came up was, why did he want the baby in the first place? These were children from quite complicated home backgrounds and Ros remembers being suddenly confronted by the possibility that they could be heading for some very sensitive discussions. She asked for any possible answers, thinking that maybe they would deal with any potential problems if they came to them, but the question was a valid one. Mike, the Teaching Assistant in the class, obviously sensed the thin ice they could be walking on, and when there were few offers of an answer he provided the memorable one of, 'Well, I think he wanted the baby to get extra child benefit because the giant who owned his house had just put the rent up.' Ros remains forever grateful for his creativity and imagination!

One of the things that kept Ros going at this stage was the comments the children made about the sessions:

- It gets your mind going and you think, Oh, I never thought of that.

- It makes you think about what it would be like if things were different.

- It makes you get inside your head and talk to yourself.

It was obvious that they too were getting a lot of pleasure from the sessions and were opening up to voicing their ideas and sharing them with others. The sharing part was quite important. Group activities often required the children to work together on a project where a model or experiment was the expected outcome. Some groups never got further than the arguments over whose ideas to choose, and although using TASC has helped them with those skills, it was initially noticeable that when the focus was purely imaginative or theoretical, the disputes did not arise. No child is going to fall out with the group over Cinderella's nail varnish or how giants can make bread from bones.

Another Step

It is not always easy for the adult to be able to keep an open mind about allowing the children to experiment. Sometimes we may doubt the validity of providing this space within the curriculum and wonder if we should be spending time on it when there is so much else to cover. The questions and responses can feel frivolous or ridiculous to adults who have been schooled to think conventionally. They may feel that it wouldn't meet with Ofsted's approval or that they can't match it to one of the week's learning objectives. These are all valid concerns. We are constrained by what we have to teach the children and it is very common for educators to worry that they are not providing children with every last detail of the many strategies and schemes of work. However, when you give children the opportunity to think creatively, discuss and share their learning you find that their interest and enthusiasm is heightened and you are not just rabbiting on to a classroom full of glazed over eyes. The challenge is to listen very carefully to the possibilities for learning as a creative process and use them to maximise the children's involvement in their learning. As the children became used to asking questions and formulating answers they began to become more thoughtful. They read *The Frog Prince* together and the responses to the questions began to evolve:

- 'What use is a golden ball?' This encouraged them to think about the value of something that is not useful.

- 'How could the frog pick it up?' One child had seen a nature programme and contested that frogs used their tongues to pick things up to which another responded that was not the same as picking something up with hands.

- 'How did she explain a frog to her parents?' Another group picked this question up as diversity was being discussed generally in the school. The connection with amphibians was swiftly left behind as they moved on to talk about prejudice and responses to differences.

- 'How could a frog live out of water for that long?' This moved them on to think about evolution and adaptation to changing habitats. That story also led to discussions about keeping promises and trusting others, and how the princess's behaviour must have made the frog feel.

Keeping a record of the early sessions proved valuable, when Ros was reflecting on what she had been doing and identifying and accounting for what she had learned and how she was improving what she was doing. Even at that early stage she can now recognise that she was becoming aware of the potential learning opportunities in encouraging children to reflect and voice personal opinions, and if necessary defend or adapt them, on a range of topics. We have all found our notes helped us to realise that learning does not take place overnight and persistence is needed. In the short term you can feel as though nothing is working and you are getting nowhere and a lot of courage is needed at times to keep going. This story is offered to you to demonstrate what took place with a class of Year 4 children, several of whom were considered quite 'challenging'. It shows what can be achieved by creative persistence over time and taking a step back to look at what is really going on, often unnoticed.

> 'Getting settled was no easy task. The room is small and we are a group of 28. I have about five "chiefs", mainly female and very vocal, to every "Indian". I distanced myself from this as they fussed about where to sit, feeling it is useless to swim against the tide. It's far better for my blood pressure and voice.
>
> Once seated we played the game of "stand up and swap places with anyone who…" which broke up the little cliques and ensured misery for some and relief for others.
>
> We then watched the wildlife PowerPoint, after which they were asked to make a personal comment or reflection. This was the first time I'd really had a chance to notice behaviour in children that otherwise is rarely seen.
>
> Charlie, who has poor literacy skills, never seems to remember anything of an organisational nature, appearing permanently "vague", was really animated and excited. So was Jasmine, a girl who can be extremely difficult in lessons and has very limited attention. Will these sessions enable them to become more confident in their own abilities and carry it into other areas which they find difficult?'
> (December 2006 Diary Entry)

Another idea that we have used to extend children's understandings between question and answer is to give them the answer and ask them to create the question. Marie, using this approach with children and adults, has found it is a fun way of beginning to explore what makes a 'good' question and creating the narrative that links the question with the answer. For instance, the answer is 'blue'. The common question that is offered is, 'What colour is the sky?' This can lead to some interesting science inquiry to check whether this is correct given our current understandings. The answer is 'round', a common question offered is, 'What shape is the world?' can lead to a historical inquiry, 'Was this always believed to be so?' It is not difficult to use this in curriculum work by asking the children to ask questions that others might ask. For example, the answer is '8', what question might a geographer ask? What question might someone who is Chinese ask?

Where to Next?

Ros went to a P4C course but found her first attempts at 'doing P4C' with her class were not particularly brilliant. The children enjoyed talking about certain topics, thought of some questions, but she found it hard to keep them on track or on time. What started off as a regular feature soon began to dwindle and fall off the end of the weekly timetable. On reflection she thinks this may have been partly due to the structured nature of a P4C session. She was not experienced enough to know how to fit the odd bits into a format designed by someone else. Time was also an important consideration; finding an odd space in the week or taking on an idea that arose in a lesson was fine. Finding a regular slot on the timetable was not. She had felt more comfortable with the way philosophical sessions had gone before. She now thinks learning about P4C and the approach that Mathew Lipman developed was very useful but it was when she took ownership of the idea that she found a way to put across what matters to her, and recognise the educational value in what she was doing.

She found that sometimes, when she felt she wasn't making headway, she had to take a step back, stop forcing something that wasn't developing naturally and give herself a breathing space. From her diary notes she can now see she did this unconsciously to start with and let the philosophical discussions drop for a while. However, such was her belief that even though at that time she couldn't 'prove it', she knew they were important to learning and, in time, with renewed determination, found a way to sneak them back in. The misfortune of a rainy playtime triggered a most amazing discussion and led her to further thoughts about the real value of working in this way.

It was lunchtime and raining. At that time her class was situated in an outside hut, cut off from the main body of the school and cramped because she had a large year group. On the bonus side was the interactive whiteboard linked to a DVD player and a supply of cartoon films in the cupboard. While eating her sandwiches and preparing for the afternoon, her class watched a recent Disney film about some rather cute racing cars. She was just about to dismiss it as typical Disney format where all seems to be lost, the hero faces a dilemma, audiences wait on the edge of their seats with baited breath and then finally all ends up happily, the hero wins and the baddy loses. Then she found herself thinking that the ending scenes would be a wonderful stimulus for a philosophy session.

The following afternoon she had the class arranged on chairs in a circle and began the session with a calming down visualisation activity. It was Friday afternoon, the children were tired from a curriculum filled week of learning objectives and it felt good to let go of such things and concentrate on something that would have no level or target, but instead required a personal opinion and ability to engage with others in discussion.

They watched the final scenes of the film again, stopping the film briefly at the point where Lightning McQueen has to make a big decision about whether to lose the race by helping an old friend, or whether to race on and win the trophy he has always dreamed of. Having made sure the children understood what the consequences of each decision could be, they then watched the final scenes.

Using the P4C structure, they then had 'thinking' time and Ros was impressed by the serious response to this. The children shared their initial responses to the film; largely about the different personalities of the cars and whether they were nice or nasty, or a mixture. Questions were formulated in small groups and recorded on a flipchart. Some children were reluctant to speak to the group but would share ideas with a partner and this enabled their opinions to be fed back to the whole class. Their level of questioning at this stage still needed to be developed, as did their ability to listen to each other, but this was something they could work on at a later stage.

After an 'omnivote', where everyone can vote as many times as they like, to encourage a confident response, it was decided that the question they would discuss was, 'Why did the cars hate each other?' Some of the responses to this question missed the point or were answers to questions not asked, so she rephrased the question, introducing the idea that the words 'dislike' and 'hate' might be two separate feelings.

If you have ever tried a philosophy session with a group of children you will recognise that this is a fairly standard procedure. There was, however, one aspect of this session that made it particularly memorable, and that concerned the response from one child. Ashley was a very quiet and seemingly shy boy. He rarely contributed to discussions, tended to let others take the lead in activities and was reluctant to engage in conversations with adults. He had arrived from Key Stage1 with slightly below average results in reading and writing and showed no great ability in numeracy or any other subject. He was a very pleasant child, but not really someone she could put character or talent to.

Ashley listened to much of the discussion that afternoon, saying very little, apart from in his small group. As the session finished and Ros asked for other questions the film had raised, his response quite took her aback. It was one of those tingle moments when you feel you've just experienced something special. Looking thoughtful Ashley asked, 'Why do people have to be nasty just because they want something badly?' Here was a child easily overlooked asking an incredibly deep and fundamental question about the nature of human beings.

This was not just a one-off incident by any means. One of the aspects of these sessions that we have come to value most highly is the frequency with which we are astonished by a child's response. This is not to say that we don't think children are capable of thinking in such depth, quite the contrary, but rather it is the very children who come out with the most profound responses that astonish. They are often not the ones with the high assessment scores or curriculum levels. They can be restless, 'challenging' and appear uninterested in their education. And yet when it comes to thinking they seem to have a refreshing originality and perception. Moreover, we have had moments feeling that real engagement with the children on a human and personal level, that their value as a member of our community of inquiry is firmly established and without doubt.

As the children develop as creators of questions and answers they become interested in finding questions to share at other times. Robert Fisher suggests a 'think wall' where questions can be put up at any time. One classroom has a pad of Post-its and a pen attached to the wall that anyone can use at any time to post a question. Everyone is encouraged to take a question they find interesting, think about it and offer an answer on a sheet they can pin up, which others can respond to or build on if they choose. This works well as it makes links with the curriculum and encourages more extended investigation and inquiry. When there is time for a session the children vote on which question interests them to explore together.

By developing their skills in creating and answering questions the children begin to realise they can themselves be the constructors of knowledge, with an ability to appraise the validity of different responses.

What we want is for all learners, adults and children, to tap into an ability to see life in a unique way. We are creating space in the curriculum where the individual does matter and is a valued part of the whole. We don't want the generations of the future, and even those of the present, to just travel along the well worn paths created by those in the past. We want to find the routes that have yet to be travelled, the ones that may provide a more effective or interesting pathway. This is one of the special qualities of the human species. We may not have the speed of a cheetah or the strength of a gorilla, but boy, are we naturally good at pulling out the stops when it comes to thinking of new and creative ideas or solutions to problems. And let's face it, life is full of 'problems' to be solved, from how to organise the living room to whether it is morally right to eat animals.

Creative and philosophical thinking is a response to problems. Each type of thinking enables us to bring our own ideas and theories into practice. Pondering what the Queen may have in her handbag may be an amusing way of passing time on a journey, but the same skills are brought into use when the problem turns to more serious topics. Enjoying and developing our own creativity, acknowledging and appreciating our uniqueness and that of others enhances life and makes the future an exciting place to head towards.

Chapter

Developing Children's Awareness and Appreciation of Themselves and Others as Knowledge Creators

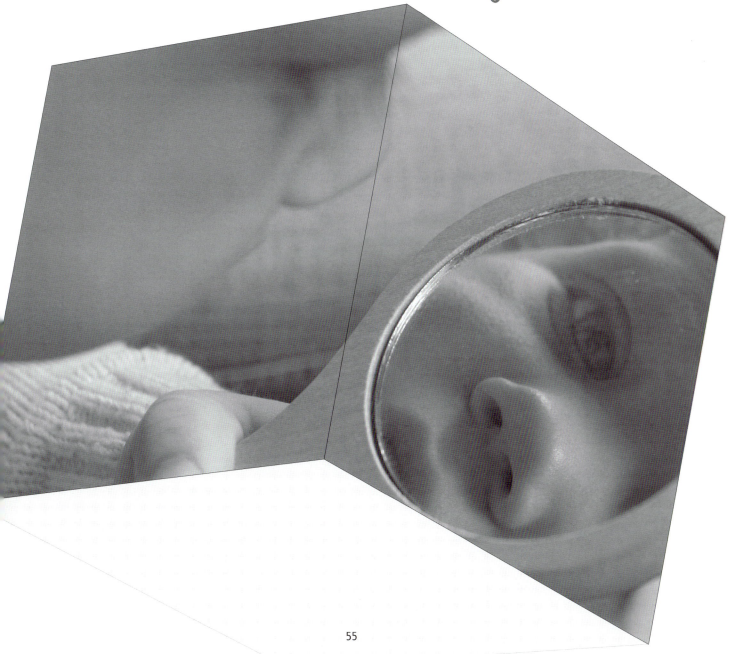

'The human mind treats a new idea the way a body treats a strange problem, it rejects it.'

Sir Peter Medawar

Why it is Important

Learning in school tends to be treated as a product, we are told to 'deliver' the curriculum. What is ironic is that we tend to remember the process of learning more than the learning itself.

Marie has had a feeling of increasing discomfort over recent years with the curriculum defined, refined and 'delivered' as universal truths. The content of the curriculum comprises the best response real, fallible people have created to questions that were of interest or importance to them and sometimes others, at a particular time. Teaching these processes should provide educational devices which enhance, not damage, children's sophistication and abilities as knowledge creators, and open their minds to the possibilities of recognising problems to address and creating new processes for knowledge creation.

The responses, the content of the curriculum, were developed as well as possible given the knowledge base and thinking of people at the time. We need to be aware that our pupils have a greater knowledge base to draw on than those whose responses they are learning about. Some 'knowledge' has survived the test of time and may continue to do so, but to present 'content' as a universal truth, is to close the minds of our future generation to the fallibility of established thinking.

Making Time and Making Links

Extra time is not necessarily needed but as educators perhaps we should be reconsidering how we are engaging children with the curriculum. A colleague distinguished between asking for 'an' answer rather than 'the' answer. What he was saying was that when we offer content as 'an' answer rather than 'the' answer we open the possibility to our pupils of creating something new and developing the skills and attributes necessary to challenge the prevailing power and 'wisdoms', opening up to the children the possibilities of creating their own knowledge (source – training day).

As we value our children's ability to create their own contributions to knowledge we become more attuned to possibilities of enabling them to work on their own ideas, share them with others, refine them in the light of discussion, and, therefore, make them important co-creators of new knowledge.

Getting Started

Developing children's awareness and appreciation of themselves and others as knowledge creators presents a challenge to the teacher in having to recognise the opportunities as they arise. Sometimes it is a simple question that will start the line of inquiry which you need to recognise, having the confidence and courage to follow the flow. Ideas will come and go and the children will have strong ideas of the path to follow. This is an example of what can happen when the teacher is open to what the children can offer.

We will set the scene for you as it is the context that is important. We all attended a Master's programme tutored by Jack Whitehead. Jack recognises and values teachers as knowledge creators and works through the master's programme to help them make their embodied knowledge public. Claire Formby, an experienced KS1 teacher who was part of the Master's group, offered this story which enabled her not only to begin to value her own knowledge but also recognise children as knowledge creators who have a wealth of their own embodied knowledge to offer, provided they are encouraged to do so. In getting started we would suggest that you might want to think about yourself as knowledge creator, the professional knowledge that you embody and how you value and share that. If you don't recognise yourself as a knowledge creator you are unlikely to recognise or value the children's abilities. We use the term 'embodied knowledge' because often we have not articulated what we 'know' but it is communicated through what we do and our whole demeanour. Claire was working with a Year 2 class and wrote in her reflective diary on 19th November 2006:

> 'We are working under test conditions, children spread out between tables, hardback books forming screens between them. A small group of special needs children is working through the test with a Learning Support Assistant outside the classroom. It is very quiet as I read out each question to the children and they then think about it and write their answers in the test booklet. It is not exactly fun but we are making the best of it!

> Then out of the blue comes an unexpected moment of creativity. The question in the test asks, 'The opposite sides on a dice add up to seven. The first picture shows one side of a dice (picture of one side of dice with three spots). The second picture shows the opposite side of a dice. Draw the missing dots on the second picture.'

> Olli's hand shoots up and I can see he is desperate for my attention. 'Yes Olli?' I say. 'All opposite sides on a dice add up to seven Mrs Formby,' he informs me confidently.

> All sorts of thoughts flash through my mind, such as 'I didn't know that and I'm 48, but then I never really bothered to look,' and 'I'm beginning to glimpse what makes you tick, Olli and why you are so good at maths.' Later, when Olli has shown the whole class that opposite sides on a dice do indeed add up to seven, I ask Olli how he discovered this. 'Well,' he said solemnly, 'sometimes I make dice out of BluTac with my brother (who is ten) and we put the spots on with the end of a pencil. Then we play with them.'

> I know I have hit on something really crucial here, something that is missing from much of my numeracy teaching, the fun and pleasure to be enjoyed when playing with numbers. The Year 2 curriculum is extensive, the pressure is great to push children to reach the next SATs level but the sacrifice is perhaps even greater. Isn't it better to know that opposite sides on a dice add up to seven?'

Claire reflecting on this incident wrote:

> 'Although in itself perhaps a minor incident, its impact on me was huge in terms of the way I now plan and teach numeracy, trying to put the children at the centre of my thinking, giving them ownership, activity, fun and enjoyment as much as possible. The incident also reinforced my understanding of how a receptively responsive relationship between child/teacher led me to this sort of development. If I had not had that kind of relationship with Olli I could have told him to put his hand down, we were in the middle of an NFER test, or I could have replied blandly, "How interesting, now onto question eight…" Probably the worst scenario is that he might not have wanted to share his knowledge with me at all if he had thought that I might

not be interested in what he had to say! Luckily for me and for him, as Goleman (2002) says, "Our relationships offer us the very context in which we understand our progress and realise the usefulness of what we're learning."'

I hope that Olli shot his hand up because he knew I valued him and therefore would value what he wanted to say. As I wrote earlier, experimenting and practising new habits require finding safe places and relationships. I feel able to be a learner in the safe space of my Tuesday group and for the children in my class.

If I'm honest I was not expecting to learn something new from Olli in the middle of a test so he also reminded me once again of the need for me to expect to learn from the children in many different circumstances.'

The class was excited by Olli's contribution and it stimulated the creation of interesting questions the children wanted to answers. For instance, they wanted to know whether he was right and asked, 'Did the sides of all dice always added up to seven?' They worked together to find ways to answer their question, bringing in lots of dice and creating tables to keep their results in. They asked other questions like, 'Why are dice made so the opposite numbers add up to seven?' and looked on the net to find out if dice from other countries are different. They asked, 'Do some numbers come up more often when you roll a dice?' Olli's contribution took the class into an extended inquiry into probability and the use of graphs. The class became so excited it was an effort to get them to leave their work to go out to play. The amount of mathematical, literacy and IT skills they practised in order to investigate and communicate the knowledge they created was extensive.'

There is so often the call for personalisation of learning and lip service is paid to the importance of learning beyond the curriculum and the knowledge the children have. The opportunity is rarely taken to value the knowledge a child has created beyond the confines of the curriculum or the classroom, or the links they make between their own knowledge and different contexts. Claire shows what can happen when a teacher opens the space for children to create new knowledge, recognise its value, help each other articulate those links and offer their thinking to others.

Another Step

As Joy became more alert to recognising the children as knowledge creators and opened opportunities for them to offer, value and work with the knowledge they and others brought and created in class, she found the ethos of the classroom changed and the roles between the children and herself became more fluid.

For instance, the Year 2 class had written poems to go in their learning logs about their thoughts and feelings of themselves. Chloe began to lead the discussion about what the children should do with these poems. Ideas bounced back and forth and Joy quietly sat back and let the children control the discussion. Turn-taking continued, Chloe pulled ideas together and assumed the lead role. The other children agreed they wanted to perform the poem before the school together, although at this point they had 30 versions. Chloe heard an idea from one member of the class about putting the poems together into one performable version. It was suggested the poem should be written up on the board and Joy found herself in the role of scribe for the class.

Chloe gathered ideas and suggested the format and style. With a lot of shuffling and help from all the class they arranged themselves and decided upon a practice. Chloe had led the group but the whole class considered ideas from everyone and they decided which were the most popular to incorporate. It was interesting to note that they decided that to make it 'fair', a line from each poem was to be included. It was a strange experience for Joy to have the lead role for learning taken by the children. She sat as an observer listening to the flow and watching the body language, and felt the glow of an educator sharing an educational space with her pupils. Joy recognised that she and her pupils had been on a tremendous journey together from the traditional role of the teacher delivering the learning, to a class of children confident to work independently and switch roles comfortably. The session lasted for forty minutes without any support through prompts or questions from an adult! More importantly, although Chloe had become the coach in the session, all of the children were focused, involved and felt listened to and played a lead part for themselves, by themselves.

The class talked about how the session had felt and linked this to their research on learning. They felt they had learned a lot about themselves and their 'places', as they changed sometimes. Don said they swapped around, meaning that sometimes Joy was the teacher and sometimes not. This opened up further and they recorded some of the roles. Karla and others agreed that initially they thought the teacher would tell them the things they needed to learn and they would practise them and then know them. They thought Joy knew everything.

But the list on the board of the roles as learners that had emerged as time went on was very interesting and different. A summary of the children's thinking is as follows:

- We are the teachers (children).
- Mrs Mounter as the teacher.
- Mrs Mounter as the learner.
- Us as the learners (children).
- We learn together, sometimes none of us know.

And finally, Anna summed up what a number of them felt when she said, 'I like learning together best, it feels nice like I am important.'

Where to Next?

'What is learning?' is a fascinating question to explore with your class and to revisit periodically to see if ideas have changed or developed. Floor books are an excellent way for the comments, photographs and work of the children on a topic to be stored. To begin one when you start exploring learning means you can go back to beliefs and ideas later and consider changes with the children. Joy used a floor book for the learning inquiry so questions and answers explored could be revisited later and reviewed. It is interesting to explore how thinking changes with time, from in the moment, to reflecting back to it. Joy's class always had several floor books running at the same time: a topic floor book, a science one and a learning floor book. This gave the children a platform to look at the best way to learn, at different times and in different parts of the curriculum. Discussions weren't planned, sometimes a time slot was set aside but the discussion or learning flowed between the children and Joy when the opportunity arose, usually from a question or comment from the children. The skill comes with time to recognise the potential of some comments and the possibilities if they are explored.

One example came quite by chance when Joy overheard a comment from one of the children. 'Why does Taz always find everything easy?' It was Joe's perception that some of the children in the class found all learning easy and they were good at everything while he was feeling frustrated that he was finding the maths task difficult. At the end of the lesson Joy put a picture on the whiteboard of Kylie Minogue. The children instantly recognised her and decided she was a great singer. By asking one question, 'Is she good at everything?' a debate was started between the children. Then Joy showed an article from an interview she had given earlier stating some of the things she found hard. The children quickly came to the decision that we can be good at some things and find others harder. None of us are the same. As a second part of this the children looked at different aspects of learning and collected pictures of people who had strength in that area. For example, they chose 'Spock' from Star Trek as a logical thinker, Jesus as loving and David Beckham for football. Photographs were downloaded from the Internet and brought in from home and added to the collection over several weeks. These were then added to the floor book.

Two weeks later during a science lesson Dani reminded Joe that he thought Taz was good at everything. Joe really smiled because he was sitting beside Taz helping him plan an experiment. Joe was confident with science and Taz found organising himself difficult. They both wrote a sticky note to add to the floor book, updating the page of photographs about learning strengths.

Initially it might feel unsettling not to have a plan or idea of how the time will develop. Joy found the responses of the children encouraged her to persevere and eventually relax, which enabled her to forge the bond of shared learning through the hesitations and sometimes the confusions.

The developing confidence of the teacher is communicated to the children and they learn to look for the opportunities and contribute to a culture that values knowledge and co-creation.

Chapter 6

Developing the Confidence and Ability to Challenge their own Thinking and the Status Quo

'A successful person is one who can lay a firm foundation with the bricks that others throw at him or her.'

David Brinkley

'Let me never fall into the vulgar mistake of dreaming that I am persecuted whenever I am contradicted.'

Ralph Waldo Emerson

'Confidence comes not from always being right but from not fearing to be wrong.'

Peter T. Mcintyre

'Life shrinks or expands in proportion to one's courage.'

Anaïs Nin

Why it is Important

Recognising that children come with knowledge they have created about the world is important. You don't challenge and progress without the confidence to at least feel the fear and do it anyway!

An example of what unexpected outcomes there can be is the story of a young Tanzanian school student, Erasto Mpemba. He had noticed that hot liquid cooled faster in a fridge than cooler liquid and wanted to know why. Despite being ridiculed by many he persisted with his inquiry, checked his observations carefully and extended his investigation over time. When Dr Osborne, a physicist from the university, visited his school he asked his question again. The academic remembered the laughter from the other students but reflected,

> 'It seemed an unlikely happening, but the student insisted that he was sure of the facts. I confess that I thought he was mistaken but fortunately remembered the need to encourage students to develop questioning and critical attitudes. No question should be ridiculed. In this case there was an added reason for caution, for everyday events are seldom as simple as they seem and it is dangerous to pass a superficial judgment on what can and cannot be.'

He went on to investigate this phenomenon himself and eventually wrote a paper with Erasto (Mpemba and Osborne, 1969) to offer an explanation for what became known as the Mpemba effect.

Making Time and Making Links

Whilst writing medium-term plans for her class Joy began looking at the content of the curriculum the children are being presented with, and also the way in which it was delivered. Does it encourage questioning of themselves and the world around them or focus more on learning subject skills and knowledge towards an attainment target? Will a child in the future look back on school and value the 'pace and challenge' they constantly experienced in all 'good' lessons?

Joy worries whether children have time to rest, to experience, to reflect or to explore learning as a skill. Will they only take away the knowledge context of lessons or will they develop the skills to articulate their own learning experiences in a reflective, emotionally responsive way, talking about the moments that were significant to them and the impact?

Will they have the vision to see forward or be caught in the cycle of maintaining the well trodden path because it is successful? How do we know it is successful? How will they know it is successful?

These questions began to concern Joy and encouraged her to explore creative and philosophical thinking with her class. She began in a small way at the start, just half an hour a week, with different activities that encouraged the children to think, play around with ideas, share ideas, solve puzzles and problems.

Getting Started

Joy was excited when she was learning together with the children in her class. They are exciting companions and look at the world through very different eyes. They talked about the research Joy was carrying out about learning. They expressed surprise that, if she was writing about learning, she didn't need their help. From the tone of comment, Jo couldn't even comprehend that Joy could write about learning without the help of the class. It made her take a step back and look at learning in her classroom from a different perspective. Their ideas were thought-provoking, challenging her thinking and helping her to see, as a learner, through their eyes. It was an important step for her to openly share with her class how she was feeling and that she wanted to explore ideas with them. Try it. Like any learning there is a sense of risk involved, a fear in moving from being the expert to becoming an equal learning partner. But the value you and the children gain from the change in relationships and expectations will surprise you.

Joy's interest in the work of Carol Dweck (2000) was an important influence at this stage. She was already interested in how intelligence is perceived and the effect this has on the way we handle learning opportunities. With the children she was able to talk about how our ability to learn is not fixed. Much depends on our ability to persevere and be determined to see setbacks as learning experiences.

Another Step

One morning four learning coaches came to work with the children in Joy's class and shared some of the poetry and pictures they had made. The learning coaches were children who had explored learning for themselves with Joy the previous year. They encouraged the children to reflect on their learning journey so far and also the journey to come. The children were then asked to make a map of their learning journey. They thought of things that could be used to show the times when learning is tricky and when it feels right. Ideas such as swamps, mountains, tunnels, traps were suggested. Other ideas included things that catch you or suck you in. When you feel positive as a learner flying free, flowers blooming, a downward slope, an open path to follow were suggested.

The maps were all different and what was so special was the explanations the children gave of the symbolism they chose. Genuine reflection and understanding of themselves as learners was demonstrated. This was the first of a series of sessions that were planned in a free way to follow the ideas of the children as researchers/learners.

The second session was very different. Picture maps were finished quickly and the conversation returned to Belle Wallace and her TASC Wheel. The children were curious as to whether lots of schools used the TASC Wheel, and for a while that thread of conversation lay quiet. Joy introduced the vocabulary of having a learning theory. This was a difficult concept for the children to comprehend and they struggled together for a while. Some still cannot explain their understanding of the discussion. From it came the idea that the children wanted to have a learning theory of their own. As experts they felt that people should listen to them and not to adults, as it is children who are the learners all day, for years as they grow. Then the quiet thread rose in a new way. 'Will they listen to us like Belle Wallace?' asked Tao – a question Joy couldn't answer. Even if others listen, will it be understood for the incredible thinking that it is, evidence of a journey and not a moment, or will it be listened to and forgotten?

The children will not forget, not for a moment. They want a conversation, a platform to talk and share ideas, thoughts, questions, to challenge, encourage and support. How can that enriching flow be created in a classroom?

Where to Next?

> 'Perhaps learning is a journey we undertake our whole lives, by realising the quality of the experiences on the journey and not the results, we learn more about ourselves and our values grow and change.'
> Wallace et al. 2004

The children in Joy's class thought about this quote for a long time, trying to understand the message she was sharing. They felt strongly that achieving the end result you want is important as well as the journey to sustain you to want to go on. But they felt definitely that through the process of research and the necessary reflection they had learned a lot about themselves and how they had changed as learners and in their self belief.

Class discussions would often tend to wander from the path that had been set out at the beginning. An example follows. The talk about theories had awakened a keen need to begin planning and articulating their ideas to form a learning theory of their own. Following the idea that TASC meant something when you looked at each letter, the children talked in pairs to find a special word of their own to summarise the learning theory. Joy was amazed as Masroor suggested the word 'quiff' quite quickly. The children liked the sound of the word and began thinking what the individual letters could stand for, just like in TASC. They didn't have to argue or even debate ideas, they quickly agreed and all ideas seemed to come from the group almost as a collective mind.

Q 'questions we all have to ask to learn'.

U 'understand – making sense of things around us and ourselves which is harder'.

I 'I am important'.

F 'feelings' so important as a learner.

F 'focus' to be able to concentrate and persevere.

'I' is in the centre, just as we are in the centre of our learning, surrounded by our understanding, questions and answers, our feelings, and the focus of our learning.

The class then decided that as TASC is represented by a circle, they needed a visual image for QUIFF. Thoughts turned to the shape QUIFF would be. The pictures are all so different and thoughtful. Below is Ali's picture. She has used a triangle with 'I' at the point, represented by an eye, the most important point, an eye to the world and into ourselves. Questions are at the bottom, the start and widest part of the shape. Focus is almost like an egg floating in between our questions and feelings that control us, our thoughts and learning.

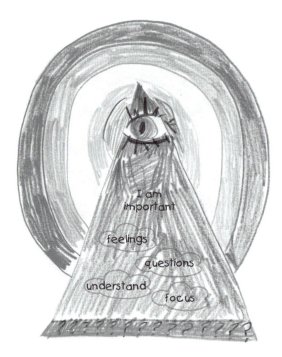

Mary Kellett (2005) highlights the opportunities for pupils to engage with a subject in great depth and work with primary, self-generated data. The depth of the children's thinking in Joy's class amazes anyone who shares the journey. Age, knowledge and skills have often been quoted as barriers to children taking part in action research, but we must challenge these preconceptions, encouraging children to critically develop their own and others' thinking.

The interactive whiteboard is a useful tool to record questions and thoughts, refining the children's ideas behind 'QUIFF'. They began thinking about how children learn best and they worked in pairs, then fours to come up with ideas, sharing them and then discussing and recording those agreed.

The children decided they learn best when they:

1. understand and use other learning skills (Paul) ('Understand' in QUIFF)

2. believe in themselves (Max) ('I am important' in QUIFF)

3. think about themselves as a learner (April) ('Focus' in QUIFF)

4. are curious (Theo) ('Question' in QUIFF)

5. are happy and calm ('Feelings' in QUIFF)

These are the five key points or rules for QUIFF which were agreed upon. Behind these are values that the children feel are important but come under the headings or rules above. Max felt not worrying if things go wrong is a very important skill, because even when things are wrong you are learning, just don't worry and keep trying (Linked to 2). Paul felt it is vital to do the right thing. Joy was unsure what he meant and asked him to explain. He said that you have to decide to be a good learner and feel right. Nobody can make you do it, they can try but only you can make it your best. Wow! (Links to number 1) April wanted included the phrase 'Don't let your dreams float away' linking to Paul's analysis of self. The bullet points are the other views that the children felt important to list.

- Mixture of learning ways for all of us (Coach Darren's group). Links to number 1.

- Concentration, only you can do it (Coach April's crew). Links to number 1.

- Belief came up again and again. Links to number 2.

- You must take learning seriously. Links to number 3.

- Help other people but also help yourself (know when to ask for help, know yourself to help yourself). Links to number 3.

- Tricky is exciting (Coach Nigel's group). Links to number 4.

- Be interested it is then easier (Coach Pat's group). Links to number 4.

- Use what you already know.

- Don't copy. Better to get it wrong and believe in yourself and just try again calmly. Links to number 5.

- Fun learning. Links to number 5.

Children have the confidence and ability to challenge their own thinking and the status quo. What we can do through using creative thinking and philosophy is help them to develop it and develop ours alongside them as co-creators of knowledge.

Chapter 7

Being Able to Create Opportunities within Constraints, Creating and Being Open to Opportunities

'I can't change the direction of the wind, but I can adjust my sails to always reach my destination.'

Jimmy Dean

'We must dare to think 'unthinkable' thoughts. We must learn to explore all the options and possibilities that confront us in a complex and rapidly changing world. We must learn to welcome and not to fear the voices of dissent. We must dare to think about 'unthinkable' things because when things become unthinkable, thinking stops and action becomes mindless.'

James William Fulbright

'Someone once told me, "Luck is when opportunity meets preparation," and that's what I really feel with my music. I've worked really, really hard on it. It was like, "This is really what I want to do… what do I have to do to make it work?"'

Erica Baxter (Australian model and pop star)

Why it is Important

Human beings are incredibly resourceful and imaginative by nature. We recognise this in the curiosity and inventiveness of young children exploring the newness of the world around them. We see it in the artistic and scientific creativity of the adult. Take a look at the developments during the last ten years in computer technology, or the changes in transport designs within 60 years, and you cannot fail to be aware and in awe of the human ability to imagine and turn the dreams into reality. This is a potential capability we are all endowed with.

And yet, as we have shown earlier, it is often the sad case that our education system fails to tap into and excite this capacity for inventiveness. Instead of this growing and developing through the experiences of formal education, natural curiosity is often lost. We work within the confines of a prescriptive curriculum overshadowed by testing, league tables and inspections.

It is not surprising then that creative and philosophical thinking can easily be crowded out by the things we will be judged on. And yet to ignore its importance is to limit the very 'potentials' that we desire our children to reach. Without providing opportunities for them to create their own learning and be involved in their own interpretation of knowledge, we create an education system that at worst only regurgitates the knowledge of the past, and at best slows down the rate at which an individual can learn.

Denise Shekerjian (1990) interviewed winners of the MacArthur Award to see if she could understand what they had in common. The award is interesting in that it can't be applied for and the winners receive money which has no strings attached. Her work is interesting to have a look at, as it throws light on those qualities common to 'genius' which are also to be found in us lesser mortals. An overview of the MacArthur Award can be found at the link below.

> 'The MacArthur Fellows Program awards unrestricted fellowships to talented individuals who have shown extraordinary originality and dedication in their creative pursuits and a marked capacity for self-direction. There are three criteria for selection of Fellows: exceptional creativity, promise for important future advances based on a track record of significant accomplishment, and potential for the fellowship to facilitate subsequent creative work.'

www.macfound.org [accessed 22/11/08]

Shekerjian found that these people shared the characteristics of being self-motivated and interested in an area, regardless of whether it had appeared in their formal education. They were creative thinkers, prepared to take risks and be ridiculed. They could cope with 'being in a fog' where their understanding was concerned, were resilient learners and had a vision of what they wanted.

We agree with Denise Shekerjian when she suggests that, 'If we cultivate a consciousness about the way we think and work and behave, improvement in our creative abilities is possible – and improvement is not something to be taken lightly.'

That space inside our heads is rather like the wardrobe in the Narnia books by C. S. Lewis. Outside it is nothing more than a container, but inside the possibilities are endless. This is the world of possibilities that we wish children to remain in touch with, continuing on into adult life. If you need even more assurance that creative and philosophical thinking is relevant to today's education and the generations of the future, then be encouraged by the opinion of Thomas West in his book In the Mind's Eye where he states, 'It is often observed that one of the essential characteristics of creativity is a "childlike" view of the world, full of freshness and flexibility… it is good to preserve something of the child, especially if we desire the freshness of view that seems to promote creativity.'

So, we need to encourage children to retain their creativity, develop the courage to explore and look for the possibilities that exist rather than be distracted by self-imposed constraints.

Making Time and Making Links

One of the most frequent barriers put up by teachers is that they say there is no room for philosophical or creative thinking, for engaging in deep and meaningful learning because the curriculum is too crowded and there is already far too much to plan for that will be assessed. We understand this concern and initially shared it. There were times when our confidence failed and we felt we could not adequately justify the time. However, the enthusiasm shown by the children, the excitement for learning together and the depth of the learning that we experienced made us return to it.

If creativity in the child is what we hope to encourage, then this depends upon the creativity of the teacher to find ways of incorporating the sessions into the timetable. The key is looking for the opportunities, believing in its value and not allowing yourself to become bogged down by planning too far ahead or creating a rigid structure within which to do it. Sometimes a time slot is set aside but the discussion or learning from it flows between the children and us and our own reflections, actions, and ideas forge the path for the next part of our journey, sight unseen.

Using Social and Emotional Aspects of Learning (SEAL) or your own personal, social, moral and emotional development programme is often where it can begin. Asking the children to consider what makes them good learners can tap into their own ideas and provide a forum for them to share them. If the focus is changed slightly, to create a 'model' of a good learner, then there is scope for creativity. We have all experienced that desire to make something rather bland a bit more exciting and many of the sessions we have run have emerged naturally from the curriculum because we have been looking for a way into a topic that we feel the children will engage with.

Initially you may prefer to start with a one-off session with a particular focus, such as seeing how many creative questions and answers you can find. Even these can be linked to something else on the curriculum. Ros's use of traditional stories was linked to a literacy unit on storytelling and fables. Joy linked her work on the TASC Wheel to a project on flight. In both cases the routine curriculum was covered, but with a deeper dimension.

Getting Started

Sometimes the opportunity to put in a creative thinking session lands in your lap unexpectedly. This is the opportunity that arises when a space appears in the timetable for which you were not really prepared. What you choose to do with that time is up to you.

There are many books available on the market giving teachers 'outside the box' activity ideas and these can be adapted to using TASC. Recently Ros spent a wonderful afternoon with her class working on the theme of alien planets. Space and dinosaurs are still popular and the fantasy element lends itself to some very creative work. Following this she wrote in her journal:

'I decided to use Outside the Box, a book of creative thinking activities. Apart from needing to get out the felt pens and find some paper it doesn't require endless resources and looks feasible with a class of 32. At least I have just enough tables although I have to find extra chairs.

I put the children into working tables of five or six per group and give out the task. They had to imagine that they were from an alien planet (too near the truth for some of them) and were writing a holiday brochure for visiting Earthlings. We went over suggestions of what could be put into this brochure, what a visiting Earthling might find useful to know, and linked it to the TASC Wheel of defining the task and "What do I know about this?" Then they went back into their groups and began to sort through the ideas they wanted to do in their particular group and who decided who was going to do what.

For the next two hours I became mainly an observer of the children, engaged totally in what they were doing, a facilitator rather than directly teaching. The room buzzed with enthusiasm. It didn't matter what general level of ability they were, the majority found a level to work at, or a way to produce their bit that suited them. Children with poor literacy skills drew diagrams and made pictures, some cut out models.

Only one group had a problem getting going and they were the children who regularly have problems sharing ideas, the ones who lack the social skills to work comfortably in a group. They'd got stuck on what to call the planet and nothing beyond that was happening, just a blossoming argument with two sides threatening to go elsewhere and not co-operate. They had great ideas and yet came unstuck with choosing the best idea. In the end it was solved by picking the name out of a hat.

The children found the lesson a creative delight. I met two of them later in the supermarket. One was still speaking 'alien' and the other, normally not interested in activities, was actually enthusiastic about the lesson and said how much he'd enjoyed it. They had been challenged by how far they could take their ideas. The less able had found a way of showing their talents.

The children were able to discuss afterwards what had made the session so enjoyable and none of it was down to excellent preparation and clear planning. The activity was allowed to flow and tap into the strengths and interests that the children already had.

- You can use your imagination and make your own decisions.
- There's no right or wrong answer so we can't fail.
- We're working in teams so there's no personal responsibility for the whole thing.
- We get to choose the ideas instead of the teacher telling us.
- Teachers can move around and talk to us about what we're doing. They don't have to stay with a certain group.'

In other sessions we have found that using TASC is an important way of allowing children to bring their own creative ideas to a project as well as their strengths. Before every Christmas some schools have a week set aside for Design and Technology activities linked to a fundraising sale. This a wonderful opportunity to allow the children to use the TASC Wheel in more depth than a single lesson can provide. An example of this is making boxes to contain sweets or fruit which could be sold at the fair for a profit.

The children can be put into groups, balancing out the strong characters with those developing as artists, communicators and logical thinkers. In the first session, focus on allowing them to discuss the task and think of some ideas, the more the better. Don't worry if the ideas seem over the top at this point, the later stages of discussion will hopefully smooth out the practical issues. This is the stage where the children should be encouraged to put all their ideas out on the table, unrestricted creative thinking. At first they may be rather apprehensive and worried that their ideas will not be 'right'. This stage will gradually disappear as they begin to realise that thinking can be fun and the purpose of the session is not a search for the one perfect result. Confidence will grow with the sharing of ideas and you will be pleasantly surprised that some of the quietest children can tap into such imagination. We have found time and again that children who may not excel in curriculum subjects have incredible imaginations and think deeply.

The next stage is to make a choice from the list of ideas by discussing the merits and drawbacks of each. Initially you may find that dominant characters and friendship alliances influence the choice, but be prepared to run with this or intervene quietly. Forceful personalities who want their idea accepted by the group will eventually have to come up with the one that works best and by discussing the effectiveness at the end you will be able to direct the children into understanding that the idea will belong to and be modified by the whole group. Success will be owned by the group and not by an individual.

It may be at this stage that you encounter problems with social skills and co-operation, but our advice is to work towards long-term results. None of us improve at anything if we give up the first time. These will not improve without the opportunities to practise them.

Once the boxes have been made, and there is scope there for individual decoration ideas, the group can then discuss the good and bad points of what they did, and what they would change another time. Over time they will become confident in reporting back to the rest of the class and reviewing the activity objectively.

Another Step

With the introduction of initiatives like AfL children are already being asked to take a more active role in their learning. Talking together about their ideas and offering constructive criticism to each other is becoming a far more common feature of classroom life.

A task such as planning an alien guidebook or working on sweet containers doesn't just invite creativity, it also demands some awareness of what things make life easier to manipulate and an understanding that essential is not the same as desirable. There is a sharing of skills as they work on producing helpful phrase books or box designs. The children are able to pool their individual experiences and come up with ideas that would work in a new context. Surely this is what life is all about, learning how to adapt and use what we already know in a new situation?

In the past we've been very reluctant in education to use this skill or knowledge co-operation. If you reflect on your own experiences at school then I doubt you were encouraged to produce a co-operative piece of work. The lesson was taught be the teacher and then individuals would work on their own ideas. These would then be evaluated and graded, pupils in competition with each other rather than joining their ideas together.

With a marking policy to update recently Ros put this idea into practice. She looked at the more official documentation on the topic and asked other members of staff for their ideas. Then she decided to ask the children in her year group what they thought about how their work was marked and whether it helped them learn. They worked in groups to a TASC format, beginning with identifying the purpose of marking and then coming up with helpful ideas. A partner teacher also did this with her class. They had less experience of working this way, but the results were the same in that the children became very involved in their contribution to the school's marking policy. In feeding back to the rest of the class both Ros and her partner teacher were impressed by the children's serious attitude and sensible suggestions.

They liked:

- having the wrong bits pointed out and explained, being shown how it could have been done
- helpful advice
- comments at the end
- house points
- encouraging comments
- being told what they need to do next
- highlighted parts of literacy assessments
- mistakes on draft copies being corrected
- spelling mistakes corrected, being able to see the right spelling
- having time to look at corrections at the beginning of the next lesson
- being asked a question about their work and having time to answer it
- marking each other's work
- advice on whether you were concentrating or working hard.

They didn't like:

- just a tick or cross
- just having the learning objective marked with a tick and so on because it didn't tell you why it was good, excellent or bad

- comments like 'well done' or 'excellent' because it didn't give you enough detail about what made it so

- when they got it wrong and there was no explanation.

Where to Next?

While a marking policy might seem to be far removed from fun with alien planets, the underlying theory is very closely linked. The children were being asked to explore ideas in both situations. They were being allowed to work in an unrestrained or confined way, by creating solutions to a problem in an atmosphere of co-operation. What the whole group produced was far better than what one individual could hope to achieve. They worked with enthusiasm in both situations. It didn't make any difference to their attitude that one was purely imaginative fun and the other had a serious purpose. The skills and open-mindedness required for each were very similar, only the outcome differed.

Being given the freedom to think without restriction as the initial introduction to solving any problem is important in that we extend our repertoire of ideas to choose from. Sometimes the most obvious isn't the best, but we will never discover that if we only keep to the tried and tested routes. Children never cease to amaze us with their imagination and inventiveness. They think of ways and possibilities that adults often overlook.

Learning in the classroom needs the input of freshness and novelty. We may be able to teach them the skills or give them access to the factual information, but it is our loss if we ignore looking at the world through a new pair of eyes.

Part 3
And Then...?

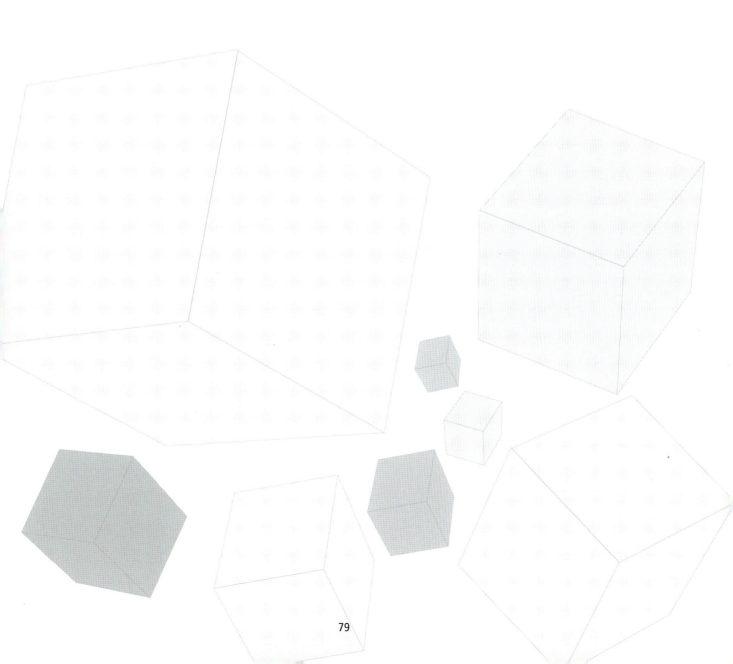

Chapter 8
Children Researching their World to Create New Knowledge

'The man with a new idea is a crank until the idea succeeds.'

Mark Twain

Why it is Important

When we talk about a child researching their world we mean, not just helping them to acquire knowledge but enabling and supporting their practise as an expert creating knowledge.

What do we mean by 'practice as an expert'? Experts don't just 'do' whatever it is they do, they are continually focusing on a problem that interests or even annoys them, on something they feel could be done better, on something that has piqued their curiosity… Whatever it is there is something that is of personal importance or interest and they want to do something about it. They explore in a disciplined manner and within a time frame in the anticipation of improving something and with the intention of creating a valued outcome. The outcome may be of value to themselves alone, such as having satisfied their curiosity, and/or it may be done with the intention of creating something with someone or something else in mind, for instance, improving the school pond as a place for frogs to live in. One way or another there is an investment of the person in what they are doing. They are focused and they engage with a passionate energy over time in the process of creating something they value.

Experts further develop their expertise through behaving as 'the expert', not by behaving as a novice. If you are learning to ride a bike you start by behaving as a bike rider and learn from the myriad of opportunities you are presented with how not to acquire bumps and bruises. You do not start by practising how to wobble around, fall off, collide with trees and break limbs. If you are lucky, another expert bike rider who has been developing their expertise will share with you some of their learning and even, literally, lend a hand. But ultimately the only one who can learn to ride the bike is the person sitting on the saddle and taking the risk of scraped knees and ego. Lance Armstrong is world renowned for his prowess as a cyclist. The quality of his early performance would be described as that of a novice and now as a virtuoso but he was and is inquiring into how to improve as a superlative bike rider, not how to become the best novice.

At first children have limited expertise and understanding particularly in the area they may choose to inquire into, but by the time a child starts school they already have an enormous amount of expertise as a learner creating new knowledge. They have learned to communicate, explore, inquire, test hypotheses, create theories, observe, analyse, synthesise, evaluate, and cognitively and critically engage to improve what they are doing. They have survived and learned from bruises, confusion, uncertainty and having to start over. They have sustained attention, persisted and have developed a wealth of expertise as inter-dependent learners and creators of valued knowledge open to the creative opportunities for deep learning. Thomas A. Edison (US inventor, 1847-1931) is reputed to have said, 'Just because something doesn't do what you planned it to do doesn't mean it's useless.' Children, from their earliest moments, learn from the unplanned, and it is there that the creative spark that we describe as 'genius' lies. They are experts in their own learning and in researching their world, and keen and eager to develop their genius.

Before they go to school many children have the opportunity to behave as an expert. They may or may not have experience of adults as skilled and dedicated supporters of their inquiries. Their sophistication may be more or less developed but even the most 'disadvantaged' child arrives in school bright eyed, bushy tailed and eager to continue, not start, their learning journeys with access to the skills, understandings and focused attention of professional educators in a space supposedly dedicated to education. They already have experience of themselves researching their world as expert scientist, artist, mathematician, ecologist… if we don't provide them with opportunities to continue to develop as expert inquirers their expertise can atrophy; like many skills it is a case of use it or lose it. Even worse, the child can lose the belief in themselves and that spark of curiosity and pleasure of being a learner can be extinguished.

Supporting children in school to continue to practise as experts, inquiring with increasing sophistication and expertise into areas of their personal interest, in a disciplined manner, with a valued outcome within a time frame, offers us as educators the opportunity to be the educational influence in their lives. That is what most of us came into education to be.

What is the distinction we are making between research and a school project or topic work? Put very simply, in the research process the intention is to create new valued knowledge, apply critically creative and philosophical thinking and to share with others what we have found valuable; whereas the purpose of a project or topic is to collect and re-present what is already known. Supporting children to research as experts offers the opportunity for them to:

- learn to challenge prevailing wisdoms and their own thinking

- gain confidence as knowledge creators

- feel the pleasure in their ability to make a productive educational difference in their own lives and those of others

- value what others offer

- appreciate through experience the fecundity of human diversity

- learn to make reasoned and reasonable decisions.

Making Time and Making Links

We are not necessarily suggesting that research should be the only learning opportunity, rather that there should be a balanced diet. What is missing in the majority of schools is the opportunity for children to research as experts.

Most of the learning in school has predetermined goals directly related to the National Curriculum. How you engage your pupils with the given curriculum is not as prescribed as some assume and by supporting your pupils to research as experts you demonstrate you are doing what the government is exhorting you to do. For instance, the following appears in the executive summary of 'Excellence and Enjoyment: A strategy for primary schools' (DfES 2003):

- **Take ownership of the curriculum,** shaping it and making it their own. Teachers have much more freedom than they often realise to design the timetable and decide what and how they teach.

- **Be creative and innovative** in how they teach and run the school.

Project or topic work is becoming more favoured again as the vehicle to 'deliver' on the targets. Within that space might be the opportunity for engaging children in determining more the specific focus of their own research. For instance, if the topic is 'The Tudors', rather than just collecting and rearranging what is thought to be known about the period, you might ask the children what sort of questions excite historians and how they could research that period as a historian. If you are studying 'light' in science you could work with the children to find out what sort of questions excite scientists and then begin to ask and seek to answer their own questions as a scientist. Chris Yapp (previously Head of Public Sector Innovation, Microsoft) asked at a National Association for Able Children in Education (NACE) conference, 'Do we need to teach our children what scientists know or to think how scientists think?' In response to this question we would say we need to prepare our children to be able to contribute fully to the rapidly changing world of the 21st century by enabling them to learn how to be expert at creating knowledge, not simply how to be expert at recycling knowledge.

Most of the work publicised about children as researchers tends to be in the realm of social science, possibly because that is the area teachers have most personal experience of. 'Learner's voice' is often the key term to look for and you will find many examples of children researching as social scientists. This can be a good opportunity to begin working with some children who have interests in that area and there may be forums already set up where this sort of research is given time and attention, for instance, contributing to the school council or the children's parliament.

If you have begun to find different times for creative and philosophical thinking as we have suggested through this book, you may decide to use some of that time to move the children to focus on sharing their research, using their skills to work together as a research group and finding forums to share their outcomes.

All schools are now expected to run extended schools activities and this is an ideal opportunity to establish a research group. The group could either be focused in a particular discipline, such as a young scientist, writer, archaeologist... or be generic. If you are feeling way outside your comfort zone, start with what you would like to do, where your research interests lie, and invite some children to join you. You may find parents or other colleagues would be interested in joining in and local universities or colleges may have staff who would be interested in working with you too. Children themselves are a resource and those who have begun to develop as researchers can improve by supporting others. Just keep in mind that the object of the exercise is not to find out what is already known but to deepen the sophistication in the process of creating credible new knowledge and in that, 'None of us is as smart as all of us,' (Japanese Proverb).

You may decide that you would like to engage with the children as collaborative researchers and work together on a shared question. If children are to gain the confidence to fly they need the opportunities to practise 'boldly going' and being self-reliant. As Guy Claxton (2002) would say, 'Spoon feeding does not develop thinking muscles.' Self-reliance and independent learning does not mean learners acting in isolation; rather, it means being prepared to take the initiative. An opportunity to be part of a collaborative research team could help the children recognise the value of diversity and the interpersonal skills they may have practised with you on the SEAL programme.

Whether the children are working on their own questions or on shared questions, it is important for everyone, especially the adults, to be respectful of the questions posed and to recognise that the most difficult part of research is in the formulation of the question. By being more respectful of children's abilities to take responsibility for themselves, their learning and their creative thinking, they might feel more respect for themselves and exercise their abilities rather than learning to be helpless. To enable children to practise skills and dispositions to research requires us to reflect on how much we do for children that they can better do for themselves. That includes resisting the urge to ask the questions for them and, instead, helping them to ask the questions that excite them. This is a skill that we as educators can usefully practise throughout the day.

First Steps

All this can seem rather daunting and at this point you might be saying, 'But I was trained as a teacher not a researcher!' Probably true. You might have to go back to your own learning experiences when you researched your world as a child to recognise that you are an experienced, if somewhat rusty, researcher. It is somewhat ironic to think that those who have most recently joined the profession are more likely to be ill equipped as researchers of their own practice. They are more likely than those who started in the less regimented days before the National Curriculum to have been through a training, rather than an educational process, on their professional course. We take heart and confidence from looking at the children we have worked with. If six year olds can do it, surely with all our sophistication and experience of the world as adults, we can. The children are delighted to have the opportunity to help us learn.

There are many different research methods you could use. The one we have found very helpful has been TASC which was developed by Belle Wallace over decades and used by educators and children internationally.

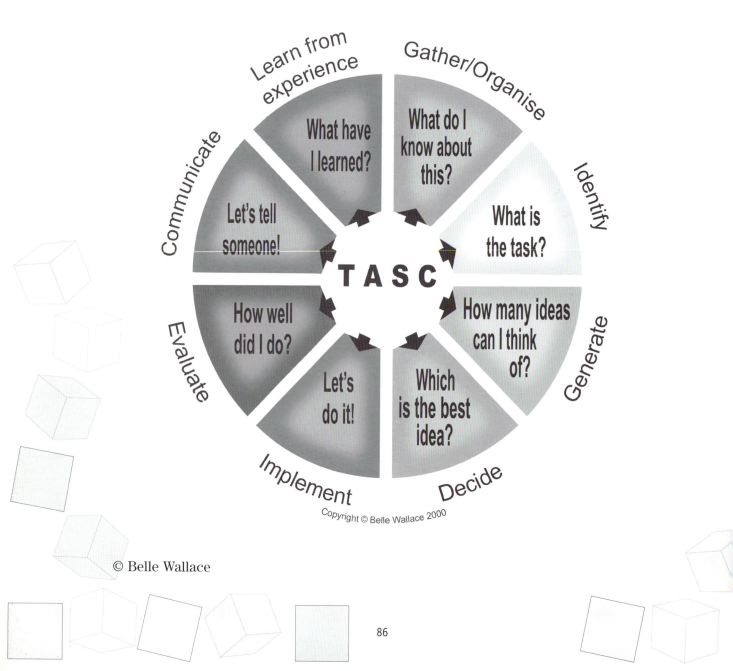

Copyright © Belle Wallace 2000

© Belle Wallace

It is 'content' free. An engineer, artist or educator all go through very similar processes. There is a wealth of material readily accessible through the web or in books and journals which gives examples of how educators working with the youngest children through to mature teachers have used it to support developing research and research skills. We do not intend to give you a detailed introduction to TASC but just a taste, which we hope will entice you to have a go. As an action researcher you might ask, 'How does developing my skills and understandings as a researcher improve my teaching?', a question which you might want to keep in mind as you research to improve your practice.

What you do now is a matter of personal preference. Some like to read about it, some want to go on a course, some like to write an action plan, some like to get stuck in and find out more and learn as they go along.

You might like to have a go now at understanding a little more about TASC through engaging yourself in a little experiential learning. We have often used this activity with teachers and children as an introduction. It can take as little or as much time as you like and it requires no equipment or preparation. It is great if you do this with other people but you can do it on your own.

Here is what we want you to do. Forget about TASC and everything else and just give this your best shot.

> The answer is 42. You can, if you prefer, have the answer as blue, a triangle, the Victorians… whatever takes your fancy. Your challenge is to come up with the best question to which that is an answer and you can have 15 minutes to do the task. The time can be longer or shorter, whatever suits. Make a note of anything you want clarification of or any discussion along the way. At the end of 15 minutes look at the questions and decide which is the best.

You may have found that you finished in one minute flat or got bored well before the end.

The common questions we have had are those such as. 'What is the sum of 20 and 22?', 'How old is my sister?' or 'What is the number of the bus that goes to town?' People feel very irritated when we say that none of them is the best because they don't make us laugh and that was our success criteria. It is amazing how often people will complete the task without seeking any clarification and then feel very irritated by being told that they have failed. No context or evaluative criteria were given in the first place so there is no way to decide, even though there was a very clear indication that criteria would be applied. We asked you to come up with **the best** question.

Now try again to come up with the best question to which the answer is an appropriate response but this time go through the TASC process, and ask questions if anything is ambiguous. Apply those creative and philosophical thinking skills. For the purposes of this toe dipping you may decide to go through systematically in one direction, but bear in mind that in a real research process you would move back, forward and between as you go deeper.

What is already known? Gather, organise and extend. I know something about the relationship between question and answer. What do I know? I know something about number, what do I know? How about number in other countries and cultures? I know that the questioner has some preconceptions about the form of question. What they are thinking of as 'best'…? As you clarify the task the best question will be the one that makes an American laugh, the best question will be the one that appeals most to a historian, the best question is the one that is the most unusual… you might want to spend a bit more time checking out what is already known. When and where do you stop gathering and organising what is already known? That is the challenge for all researchers, to describe the scope, what is pertinent to their inquiry and what to leave as a distraction, what to include which will enrich, to check where knowledge claims being made are unsubstantiated… As an educational researcher it is interesting that teachers often do not like to spend time gathering, organising and extending their knowledge about what is known, yet this is one of the main tasks set for children. The purpose of projects and inquiries is usually to entice children to want to find and organise 'facts' uncritically that are predetermined and part of the curriculum, and present them attractively either for the wall or in a test.

What is the task? Check out if you need any further clarification. When you complete the task how will you know you have done so successfully? What data might you want to collect to enable you to provide evidence? For instance, if the best question would be the one that makes us laugh the most, will we want to record responses on a laughometer, or by a show of hands, a video of the bodily responses? If you are thinking, this is too hard, for goodness sake what is the point, it might help to reflect on how often children are told that we want them to do their best and then collect data, in the form of test results, which is then used to show their underachievement.

Back to the TASC process. Having clarified the task, take your time and come up with as many creative imagined possibilities as you can. For instance, are you going to present your question in mime, dance, poster, orally…? Considering we say how important it is for children to be encouraged to be creative and how much employer's value creativity, it is ironic that children and adults often need a lot of encouragement and practise to really let their imagination work freely.

Decide which idea you are going to use. Check out how you decide and what criteria you actually use. What often happens is the last one that is offered gets chosen, or the loudest, or the most polished. In life it is not unusual for the decision to have been made before the task was set.

Then there is the 'do it' phase. This is the phase that is usually easiest for people to work with. It is here that you develop and apply project management skills such as managing risk and creative problem-solving when things don't go as planned, recognising the good fit between people and tasks to allocate the work. Some talents that often go unappreciated, for instance, those of the informal leader, team worker, motivator and so on, might be recognised, particularly when the proponents are not present!

Having completed the task, you move to the evaluation phase. You were set the task, 'Come up with the best question to the answer 42.' You need to put your response to the test and evaluate against the criteria set. How good is it? How well did you do? What might have improved the response? How might you want to modify the task in the light of experience? Would you now modify the success criteria?

Next is the 'communicating to others' phase. You could look on this as the phase where you begin to create your research account, describing and explaining the whole process to share the knowledge you have created. You do not just review the task, you focus on the process of knowledge creation you have been involved in. As you begin to communicate with others about this you will find your thinking goes much deeper. Between you, you will begin to analyse and learn from what otherwise you will have disregarded as important or trivial. Creating an account that communicates beyond the immediate moment is not just important to enable others to learn from your experience and thinking; it requires clarity of thinking that opens possibilities for profound and wise learning. What is often missing in these accounts is the theorising. Just a description of what has happened is of little use. It is the theory offered, the 'why' that takes you into the creation and offering of new knowledge that can contribute to us all making progress, rather than continually rehearsing the past.

The 'last' phase of the TASC is also one rarely attended to in detail and is the other phase where deep learning happens. What have you learned about the process of learning and yourself as a learner and knowledge creator, your skills and understandings, your world, your passions, interests, motivations, values? We will return to this in the next chapter.

This has been a quick introduction to the TASC process. It is not surprising that children improve their written and oral communication skills, their high level thinking, their interpersonal skills, their ability to work independently and interdependently and their appreciation of themselves as capable learners when they engage in researching to create knowledge they value.

You may decide that you can only occasionally give the children the opportunity to behave as expert inquirers but there are numerous opportunities to practise and enhance the skills that the children draw on. We have found it very helpful to have the TASC Wheel up on the wall to refer to. We have also found it useful to make a large copy, laminate it and cut it up, and put BluTac on the back of each section so that we can take a section down to emphasise the connection between what we are doing in a lesson and how they might use those skills at other times. For instance, if the children are doing a project, we might have the 'gather and organise' on the wall as we talk about the questions they are going to explore on the Internet. We might have the 'What is the task?' and the 'What have I learned?' sections highlighted as we have a philosophy for children session.

The TASC Wheel has many forms that will be suitable for children of any age from Reception onwards. They can be as simple or as complex as necessary – hard copies on the wall, small copies that rotate with a split pin in the centre or laminated as part of a planning board. You can gradually expand the picture of TASC as you and the children progress. This is an example of a version that Joy created with her six year old pupils.

'The class quickly made a large wheel which was kept on the classroom wall. It was initially used a lot but soon the flow of the segments became integral and embedded within our thinking. We started with a topic focus inquiry week using the wheel to plan and implement throughout the week. This enabled us to see all of the segments of the wheel working and supporting each other in a small time frame. It enabled everyone to be involved, to clearly understand the steps we were taking, but didn't contain our creative learning. Rather it allowed us to fly, but gave us the vocabulary and ideas as prompts if required.'

Another Step

Visiting and working with other schools can be exciting and a good way to gain new ideas and share concerns. It is also an opportunity to spread the cost of inspiring trainers and share expertise. Joy, having found out about the TASC Wheel, wanted to introduce it to her class in a way that they would be able to remember over a short space of time. Planning and using the wheel during a term would lose the impact and flow of the segments for the children. A project was developed with several schools. The main intention of the project was to introduce and gain confidence in using the TASC Wheel as a cluster. Training was planned on different aspects of developing thinking and creative learning, including concept mapping and the TASC Wheel. A week was booked in all the schools for a special project to be planned by the teachers and the children together, using the TASC Wheel.

Many topics for the week were suggested which would inspire teachers and children, and were general enough to be interpreted in many ways. In this instance 'Taking Flight' was chosen.

Each year group across the cluster of schools took a different focus, for example, bubbles in Reception, hot air balloons in Year 2 and space travel in Year 6. Other themes were 'taking flight of imagination' for writers, 'designing the best paper airplane' for those into technology and designing a pamphlet on bird spotting for the environmentalists. By taking a clear, focused time frame such as a week it enabled Joy to introduce the TASC Wheel to her children and work through the different segments while they were still fresh in the their minds. The experience linked like-minded teachers, highlighted expertise and opened Joy's mind to the potential of creative learning.

Joy's Reflections on the Project

'As part of the 'Taking Flight' project we worked in phase groups from all the schools and made our plans together. Many trips were planned for all the children in one year group across all the schools. For example, all the Year 6 teachers chose space travel as their theme. A trip was planned to @ Bristol and the Eye Max theatre. Year 4 studied birds and all the schools visited Chew Valley Lake together. Many exciting topics and activities were planned with the children using the TASC Wheel. My class communicated with others through our class assembly to all the parents, but we also took part in the Chew Valley Enterprise Fair. This was an exhibition sponsored and supported by local businesses. We had a stand there to promote our work through the 'Taking Flight' topic and the TASC Wheel we had used.

This was such a success that we decided to introduce Thinking Skills weeks throughout the year based on different curriculum areas. Each topic was based and planned by the children following the segments of the TASC Wheel. We tried the theme weeks termly, six times a year, but found this was too much. Following the old terms of three times a year worked much better. Themes have included, problem-solving weeks, being healthy, taking flight and water. Different co-ordinators take it in turns to plan the week, as an individual school or as part of a larger project as a cluster. Maths and Literacy are still taught in the mornings, but the curriculum is dropped in the afternoon and the topic developed. Be creative with groupings, try family, mixed groups or work stations the children rotate through. A lot is gained by working with children and adults you are unfamiliar with or in a different environment. Whether you can tie in your work with an exhibition or just share what you have done with each other, the reflection and evaluation of the project, your learning skills and yourself as a person are all very important. Take the time to really focus on the evaluations and reflections you make. This is the key to developing your thinking and your understanding of yourself.

From that week the children and I saw the value of and loved using the TASC Wheel for its simplicity if we needed it, but also the layers of thinking it encouraged and challenged us to use. Soon the wheel became the framework for all of our work, even if not explicitly talked about it had become so embedded that we talked and planned using the format with confidence. Its uses were quickly found for short planning of topics, termly topic plans, science or any area of the curriculum. Sometimes we used the wheel as a whole, or smaller parts of it for focused evaluation. The children felt more confident knowing it was on the wall and actually saw it as a resource if they were 'stuck', often looking at the flow of the segments and focus questions on the inner wheel to help them. I asked the children to record the ways they could help themselves if they were stuck and in most children's work the wheel was included as one of the first ways they thought of. This activity is useful for all children to really focus on strategies to help themselves and each other as independent learners. Part of this is knowing that there are some questions without definitive answers, and that sometimes there are questions or problems we cannot solve.'

Where to Next?

Once you begin trying to teach more creatively and include thinking skills it opens your mind is opened to look at, critically, the systems and frameworks you are working in. Often individual schools will interpret the curriculum and timetabling issues in different ways. There is no right or wrong way as long as it feels right and works for you and your children. Many of the QCA units are good, but others are dry and less than inspiring. If a teacher is not excited teaching them, the children will not be excited learning from them.

Joy felt restless with the curriculum and plan of her week. Trying to make natural links between units and not worrying if they were in different year groups can make topics. For example, it seems logical while studying Ancient Egypt to link Joseph's Coat for Design and Technology and the Nile as a river for geography. Playing around with sticky notes and sheets of paper is a good way to start by grouping art, D&T, history and geography. Basing your curriculum map on skills means that it doesn't matter what year group the unit is meant to be in. Adjusting the key questions and skills required is all that is necessary. Some of the units can be linked to local resources or places to visit, giving strength and interest to a theme.

Once the topic themes have been created and agreed subject leaders can then write unit guides for each theme. These highlight the core subject skills to be covered, resources, questions and prompts. Assessment grids can be created for all subjects based on the same format. These need to be specifically designed to be completed in a few minutes and be accurate but not onerous. They identify the skills, values and attitudes for the unit and the teacher identifies, within three levels, those above and below expectations for their year group and those not listed are on target. These feed back to subject leaders with information about resources needed, websites found that were useful or comments about the skills.

These changes can make time management easier. This opens the possibility of having two afternoons each week as Topic Time, covering the four areas identified, that is, history, geography, art and D&T. This worked extremely well for Joy, making her planning easier and making natural links for the children that helped understanding and learning.

Linking the changes to the planning and the children's confidence using the TASC Wheel seemed the next step for Joy and her class. Involving the children more in reviewing what they already know at the beginning of a topic links clearly to planning for the topic and completing the class medium-term planning. This also brought another strand of Joy's learning journey together by using this together as the first few pages in the class floor book:

- We already know…

- Questions we would like to answer…

- Ways we can find information…

- Activities that would help our learning…

Creating an atmosphere of shared learning isn't easy in a classroom. It is a challenge to step back and wait sometimes. Often Joy will have just half an hour in a busy week to focus on learning. The children have 'Thinking' books which aren't marked in the normal way, more a sharing of ideas, thoughts and comments. They are used for all sorts of tasks, problems, mind maps, poems, anything generated from these sessions that should be recorded and odd ideas or 'finds'.

Joy was working with the children on developing perseverance when working alone and in a group. Finding sayings or examples of famous people really persevering over a long period can inspire everyone. Web sites are a good source and often have search bars you can use. These are some examples that Joy used with her class as talking points:

- I readily absorb ideas from every source, frequently starting where the last person left off.

- Genius is 1% inspiration and 99% perspiration.

- The three things that are most essential to achievement are common sense, hard work and stick-to-it-ness…

- I have not failed. I have just found 10,000 ways that do not work.

- Research scientists often develop ideas over a long period of time, sometimes even a lifetime.

Puzzles that encourage the children to think in different ways, play around with ideas, help develop questioning skills, as well as think creatively and co-operate with others, can be fun. The puzzle below confounded the children through a wet lunchtime until one pair quietly sat in a corner and made a paper boat, animals and corn, and began trying to physically move the items back and forth across the river. The model was left until the next day when they began trying to solve it again. Suddenly that sense of shared joy and pleasure rippled through the room as they hugged and ran to tell Joy. The sense of pride and pleasure encourages and inspires future learning and sense of worth.

This is the puzzle the children solved:

A man has a fox, a chicken and a bag of corn on a river bank. He only has a small rowing boat to cross to the other bank. The boat will only carry the man and one other item at a time. If he leaves the fox and the chicken together, the fox will eat the chicken. If he leaves the chicken and the corn together the chicken will eat the corn. Oh dear!

How can he get them all safely across the river in his rowing boat?

It encourages shared discussion and working together. Part of this can also be knowing when to give up and that some problems cannot be solved!

Joy found the more she set picture puzzles, mazes, problems and odd questions for the children to think about, the more confidence they gained and the more creatively they began to think and question the world around them.

Chapter 9
Children Researching Themselves

'The principal goal of education is to create men and women who are capable of doing new things, not simply repeating what other generations have done.'

Jean Piaget

Why it is Important

Through this book we have explored attributes we believe to be important for children to develop, to help them live lives they find satisfying and productive. We have given practical examples of how we have used creative and philosophical thinking to enhance their development. In Chapter 8 we talked about the importance we attach to children recognising themselves as able learners, influential in their own learning and that of others, and how we might provide support and opportunities for them to develop the life skills and understandings as experts researching to create valued knowledge of the world.

We have asked ourselves what we should do to improve the quality of education for our children. Our thinking took us beyond just supporting children exploring and creating knowledge of the world, to include supporting them in exploring and creating knowledge of themselves in the world.

As children learn the skills we believe are important, such as literacy and numeracy, they are also learning about how to learn, about themselves as learners and how they inter-relate with others. What they also learn, although we rarely recognise that we are teaching them, is to create stories to account for the person they are and how they want to live their lives. In the previous chapter we talked briefly about how we might help children improve their ability to tell stories through which they form, reform, and re-form their beliefs and theories to create and offer new knowledge about the world. In this chapter we want to focus on the stories children create about themselves and how we might enhance their ability to create generative, transformational stories and become more sophisticated in being an educational influence in their own learning and lives through extending their research to include themselves.

As children we create stories about ourselves. We formulate hypotheses, gather evidence and test them. We develop our values, those ideas about what is important to us, which form standards by which we judge our lives as satisfying and productive. We decide what aptitudes we have, where our passions and interests lie, what motivates us and we formulate theories about ourselves which can inform what we do. We rarely do this systematically or deepen our understandings through creating research accounts.

Carol Dweck (2006) provides an example of how influential our self-theories are. She talks of two theories of intelligence that she has found people have which have considerable implications for how they engage with the world and their psychological wellbeing. A fixed mindset describes a theory of intelligence as an attribute we cannot change. A growth mindset describes a theory of intelligence as an attribute that can be learned and improved. The implications are extensive but an example is their response to tasks and situations which are challenging. People who accept the label 'gifted' with a fixed mindset will tend to treat failure as something to be avoided because it challenges their self-image as 'gifted' or 'intelligent'. Those with a growth mindset tend to treat failure as an opportunity to learn to become smarter and will engage with relish. Those who accept the label of 'not gifted' with a fixed mindset will engage with challenging tasks without anticipation of success. As that well-known phrase attributed to Henry Ford explains, 'If you think you can or you think you can't, you are probably right.'

As teachers we contribute to these stories of self whether we intend to or not. You can test the truth of this assertion by thinking back to your own school days and exploring what you remember of the energising and optimistic as well as negating and damaging influences you experienced. Think back to when you were young. What were your learning sparks, how did those sparks happen, how were they fanned or extinguished? Don't just think in the abstract – try to describe actual moments and the people involved.

Marie has asked those questions many times in workshops and frequently there are descriptions of the adult who seemed to take a real personal interest in the child, or who let their own passion or delight in what they did shine through, which resonated long after. Sometimes the connection was made for just a brief moment but the influence was for life. Mr Donaghue who made Peggy feel she could 'do art', Mrs Hughes who insisted that Sam join the hockey team where he found he really enjoyed improving his abilities as a team player and his physical skills, Miss Taylor who made nearly everyone who came anywhere near her passionate about science.

They remember the person who believed in their ability to learn and their ability to contribute something of value. They felt recognised as a real person and not just a member of a class or a group. They felt respected as having something of worth to contribute. Whatever it was, it taught them something of themselves as the person they were and wanted to be. As Francis Fukuyama (1992) said, 'Human beings seek recognition of their own worth, or of the people, things, or principles that they invest with worth.'

John Dewey (1916) said, 'Education is a social process; education is growth. Education is, not a preparation for life but life itself.' This preparation to have an educational influence on themselves and in the world is not something that can be left to chance or wait for the child to leave school. As we have said, it doesn't in fact wait and our children learn as much by how they learn as by what they learn, and they learn about themselves through that process.

How and what we recognise teaches our children about what we value, which can inform their thinking and feelings about themselves for life. Sometimes we attend to our contribution towards this aspect of the children's learning. Rarely do we actually seek to help them develop these skills and understandings explicitly and as a result many people leave school having little appreciation of the person they are and want to be, and what it would be for them to live a life they find satisfying and productive.

For the most part the knowledge we create about ourselves as we grow up, our values, beliefs, theories, aptitudes, aspirations, talents, motivations… are left to grow in a dark place without challenge, unfortunately often nourished by self-defeating stories of negative experiences. It is with the intention of bringing these stories into the light, so we can support children to develop their educational influence in themselves, that we have begun to explore how we might help them to research themselves and tell their research stories.

We want to help children to learn to tell a particular type of story, stories that are educational and generative. We can learn from other professionals. For instance, Kobus Maree (2007) describes the influence of these sorts of stories which are developed between client and career counsellor using a narrative approach.

> 'In telling their stories, clients come into closer contact with their life experiences. Furthermore, telling expresses meaning and makes that meaning evident to both client and counselor. As clients tell their stories, their lives start to add up. Story by story, they build the architecture of a larger narrative. Slowly they begin to

consolidate narrative lines as they recognise the repetition of themes and, in due course, identify the underlying logic of the progression. As they make implicit meanings more evident, they evoke wider dimensions of meaning. Then they may elaborate and revise these dimensions of meaning to push back constraints and open new space for living. This revised narrative states what they already know about themselves and reorganises it into a life portrait that honors intuition, stirs the imagination and reveals intention. At the beginning of counseling, many clients are strangers in their own lives. At the end, they are able to use work to become more whole as they infuse their projects with their own purpose and plans.'

The description of the role of the counsellor and the teacher seem to have a great deal in common and we believe that we can help children become less like 'strangers in their own lives' by teaching them how to begin to create their own living educational research stories of their lives as they live them. The skills and understandings that are developed through creative and philosophical thinking are amongst those that are key to telling such stories.

Philosophical questions such as, 'What is learning?', 'What is the purpose of education?', 'What is it to live a productive life?', 'What is it to live a satisfying life', 'How can I improve what I do?', 'What is really important to me as principles to live by?' are not just of concern to adults. We might phrase the questions differently depending on the vocabulary and language of the children we are working with, but irrespective of their sophistication, children develop their own understandings and their own implicit theories, which will reflect in their engagement with the educational experiences we offer and what they learn through life. We think education is about helping children to improve the stories they tell to explain their world and the life they want to live, able to learn from the past, plan for the future and live in the present.

Skills of good story telling include creative and philosophical thinking to imagine possibilities to plan for the future and to learn from the past by analysing and weaving credible connections between experiences and understandings that frequently seem unconnected. What is often missing from these stories is 'living in the present' and researching to test the theories created.

Winslade (2007) shows how important it is not to just help stories to be told but to help people learn to tell and hear their own.

> 'The assumption here is that the representation of an event or object, the story of it, plays a role in creation. Stories should not be dismissed as either neutral mirrors or biased perspectives. Narratives play a part in producing a reality. Stories affect people's lives. They are not just reports of life. Hence, in counselling we can work directly with the narrative in order to have an effect on the way a story is lived out. The task of career counselling then becomes one of eliciting a person's narrative of meaningful action in the world.'

The stories that children create about their lives can change and in changing can change their lives. We have been working towards helping children create transformational stories about the possibilities of the lives they want to live through a form of living research, building on the skills and understandings they have of researching the world through a TASC process.

Making Time and Making Links

'Every Child Matters' is a core government initiative, which was heralded as a new approach to the wellbeing of children and young people from birth to age 19.

The Government's aim is for every child, whatever their background or their circumstances, to have the support they need to:

- be healthy
- stay safe
- enjoy and achieve
- make a positive contribution
- achieve economic wellbeing.

This means that the organisations involved with providing services to children from hospitals and schools to police and voluntary groups, will be teaming up in new ways, sharing information and working together, to protect children and young people from harm and help them achieve what they want in life.

DfES (2004) *Every Child Matters: Change for Children in schools*. London: Department for Education and Skills.

By devoting some time and effort to enabling children to research themselves we are contributing overtly to their emotional and psychological health and safety, enabling them to learn what brings them pleasure and a sense of achievement, begin to understand what positive contribution they can make to their own lives and the lives of us all, and what they might find satisfying and productive when they have to earn a living.

The increasing focus on strategies, such as inclusion and personalisation of learning and the launch of the SEAL programme, gives further encouragement to teachers and schools to improve the teaching and learning in the affective domain.

The approach we have taken, extending the TASC process means we help them to recognise explicitly what they are learning as they focus on learning skills or content in the curriculum, or on creating knowledge of the world.

Getting Started

It is not a case of starting something new but rather being more tuned to recognising opportunities as they arise. For instance, as Joy and her pupils became more confident exploring learning skills and using the TASC Wheel, they became more dissatisfied as well. One of her pupils, Philip, described the wheel as too flat, too two-dimensional. Joy asked him to say a bit more and he said, 'My thinking spirals around, flowing over the edge of the circle and up through the middle of the wheel and explodes, sometimes showering others with sparks from my learning.'

The class thought about what he said and after a little more class discussion Joy asked them to tell the person next to them how they described their learning. She then gave them the task, for homework, of putting their thoughts on paper. She told them they could write in any way they liked, a piece of description, a poem, or they could draw their thoughts and label the drawing so everyone could understand. They were told that if they continued the task for homework their work would be put up on the wall so they could all see what ideas other people had come up with. As children brought their work back and the display was extended others got ideas about what they might do. Some children took their work back to improve it by extending their writing and elaborating their pictures so the other children could understand more about what they were thinking.

The following week the discussion was continued. The class eventually decided they liked the idea of describing the process of their learning as a wheel which was like a cushion, with no outer edge, more of a curve below spiralling their thinking up through the middle, as though you could never quite be in the same place again. Some of the children wanted to build a model to show what they were thinking. This is a photograph of the wheel the children developed from their experiences and reflections as learners.

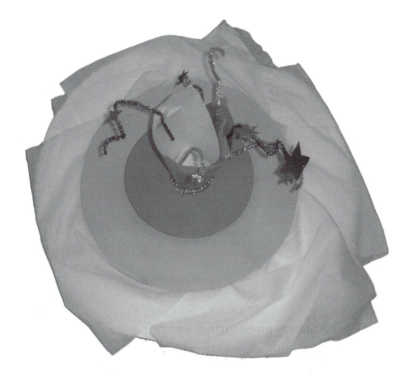

Model of the children's own Thinking Wheel

The children extended their description of their learning theory as they built the model. They explained that the colours (they chose yellows ranging to orange) were important. They had to be bright and exciting, like their learning, with the deeper orange in the middle and the gradations to the lighter yellows as it flowed over and under and then burst up through the middle again to shower the sparks of what they had learned onto the new learning.

Another Step

Once an open, safe space to ask questions is established, the strangest, funniest and most thought-provoking questions can spring up. Often all that is required is the confidence to allow the questions and discussions to roll. Sometimes activities are requested because of the discussion and the only constraint can be time. Joy's class began asking more and more questions about themselves and how they learn. The more they inquired the more everyone shared their thoughts and the more positive the children's perspective of learning appeared when they wrote personally. Curiosity about learning may lead to questions about memory, the brain, forgetting things. These are just a few of the questions Joy's class asked each other:

- How do I store the learning bits?
- Do I stop learning?
- Can I switch learning off?
- How do you feel when you are learning?
- Does my brain get hot when I think hard?
- Where do things go when I forget?

Questions about all sorts of issues become important and interesting to play with. Joy was asked one morning by Flora, 'Why do roses have so many petals?'

Several children thought carefully and ideas ranged from, 'To keep caterpillars dry when it rained,', 'So that we have lots of petals to make perfume,' and, 'Because God thought they should be the prettiest flower.' The children were all happy sharing ideas and valued each contribution, thinking it through, sometimes accepting it as an idea or asking a question to offer another viewpoint. Joy asked the same question at a staff meeting to demonstrate how the children were thinking creatively and sharing ideas. Joy's question to adults met with silence initially and then, 'I don't know,' from everyone. Adults sought what they thought was the correct scientific answer. When not finding one they didn't know what to say.

While working with Year 6 Joy was presented with an article from the paper about schools in the future. A simple clipping had interested Nick so much that he was curious what Joy thought a school would look like in 10 years' time. The children all had lots of ideas and suggested independently that they could work in small groups and plan a school. Often one small question asked at the right time, sometimes by a teacher but often by a child, can trigger a whole new perspective. Katie asked if it would still be called a school or something else. This opened up a lot of new ideas and the children not only planned their learning space, but presented it to each other when they had finished. Important features that occured in lots of plans were taken and shown to the headteacher.

We do not think something magical happens when you become an adult. By the time children get to school they already have an enormous amount of embodied knowledge and their own theories to account for their learning and the world. They may not be able to articulate them well, they may not be particularly logical, rational or reasonable, but that doesn't seem to be unique to childhood. The challenge to teachers is how to enable children to recognise their own abilities to think for themselves, to have the confidence to put their creative ideas out there, to value themselves as creative, capable thinkers and to overcome the inevitable personal and emotional challenges.

Where to Next?

One late Friday afternoon towards the end of a long term Ollie asked Joy if he could make his 'learning me'. Ollie wanted to make a model of himself as a learner. Joy was intrigued and talked to him with the class to find out what he wanted to do. He described carefully what he imagined and what they would need to do. The children were excited and immediately began planning.

His idea was quite simple for us to organise and the children quickly raided Joy's stock cupboard. Without any intervention from an adult or further planning, the children laid large sheets of paper on the floor and carefully began drawing around themselves in pairs. They cut out their paper images and began turning them into their learning selves.

Discussing what they were doing was fascinating as they continued to work, very clear about what they wanted to achieve. Collage materials were used to create parts and effects. Idea baubles, sacks to store them in, pipes for them to whizz along, were made. Hearts full of their families, circled by friends, cats to show curiosity and even information dripping out of the souls of James's feet, were included. The children were all working independently, all couldn't wait to start and certainly didn't have any problems deciding what to include. The outlines soon began to fill up, but the children were quick to explain and label the different parts. Joy used photographs and video clips of the session to play back to the children to highlight some of the good learning and for the children to feel the sense of success and pleasure evident when they were working.

Chapter 10

Teachers, Developing your own Story

'…we do research to understand. We try to understand in order to make our schools better places for both the children and the adults who share their lives there.'

Eliot Eisner

Why it is Important

In bringing our own creative and philosophical thinking into what we do in our teaching we are admitting to our own fallibility, which opens us to leading the learning in the classroom by authentic example. We are inviting our pupils to learn with us the skills, and gain the confidence, to develop their own rational understanding of what is right and reasonable and withstand the imposition of thought and behaviour by those who have 'power over them'. We are not just modelling 'good learning'.

We believe it is as important for adults to engage in creative and philosophical thinking as it is for children. Thinking is not just for childhood, it is for life. As we do battle to stay afloat on the wave of initiatives, strategies, targets and league tables we need to be asking questions such as:

- 'What is important to me?'

- 'What is it that gives meaning and purpose to my (professional) life?'

- 'How do I make decisions about what to do with my pupils that adds to the quality of their educational experience with me?'

- 'Why choose this approach rather than that?'

While such questions may not be consciously thought about all the time, our answers to them affect what we do, or should do, if we are to hold ourselves to account as professional educators.

A lot of 'thinking' is treated as though it is simply a cognitive exercise. Victor Quinn (1997), as he finishes his book, acknowledges the connection between head and heart when he says:

> 'I have taken pains to emphasise the intellectual by contrast with the academic, but not with the affective. The connection I see between cognition and affection is so close that I do not value any cognitive achievement that is not seen by the achiever to rest on feelings. All values, including truth itself, exist in an important respect as response to our feeling needs.'

In creating our living educational theory research stories (Whitehead and McNiff, 2006) we connect head and heart.

The stories we are concerned with here are educational research stories that focus on improving what is really important to us, what drives us as educators. It is where we get the feeling of satisfaction in our work and why we want to improve what we do. The stories of our improving educational practice are not just descriptions of what we do. Creating educational research stories helps us clarify our values and beliefs, which are often implicit, and we show how they influence our practice as we explain why we do what we do and make judgements about improvement.

> 'Beliefs are what we hold to be true. Values are what we hold to be important.'

> 'What we value and believe has an impact on how we behave and the choices that we make. It is therefore very important that practitioners examine their values, beliefs, attitudes and opinions and consider how these may affect their practice.'

DfES (2007)

In traditional research in education there tends to be no reference to values. Often the very qualities that make us want to work with children, such as their energy and enthusiasm and the quality of the educational relationships we develop with them, seem to be excluded from the process and accounts. This might be one of the reasons there is reluctance by teachers to research their practice. They see research as having little to do with their real experience of the classroom or why they are passionate about improving what happens for children in school. A lot of time is spent in dealing with administrative and bureaucratic processes and being trained in delivering the curriculum which can sap the will to teach, let alone research the practice. In creating living theory research stories you are focusing on your creativity, respecting your own professional knowledge and the development of educational relationships with your pupils that make an important difference, which can help revive flagging spirits. That has been our experience. We agree with Sir Peter Medawar (1969) when he said:

> 'The purpose of scientific inquiry is not to compile an inventory of factual information, nor to build up a totalitarian world picture of natural Laws in which every event that is not compulsory is forbidden. We should think of it rather as a logically articulated structure of justifiable beliefs about nature. It begins as a story about a Possible World – a story which we invent and criticise and modify as we go along, so that it ends by being, as nearly as we can make it, a story about real life.'

'Educational research focuses on our values that give meaning and purpose to what we do,' (Whitehead, 1989). They are the values we use to account for our professional lives as we live them. The evidence of them in our practice should communicate, in our research, the healthy energy, enthusiasm and wellbeing that are experienced within educational relationships of quality. By making our educational research stories public, other people help us improve what we are doing. We offer our research accounts as educational gifts to others.

We understand educational research as a process of creating transformational research stories; that is, they help us improve what might be and not simply to prove what has been. Creating our living theory research stories is really transformational Continuing Professional Development (CPD)!

Making Time and Making Links

What we are concerned with here is focused on what you are doing in your classroom and school, so the time that you make is the time for you to really look at what you are doing, to reflect and think. We know that this makes good sense, but often the urgent gets in the way of the important. It is really rather perverse that time to think, in our action-orientated society, is often looked on as a luxury. This is not helpful as teachers often feel guilty for taking time to think. This gives very odd messages to our pupils as they experience us as 'living contradictions' and adds to our feelings of stress as we experience ourselves as 'living contradictions'.

It might help you to preserve and maintain the time you have if you list for yourself why it is important to you as a professional educator. Think of how to say this with confidence to yourself and your colleagues. For instance:

- It is important because I am finding out how to improve what I am doing educationally.

- It is important because I want to be sure that I am not inadvertently causing collateral damage while acting with the best of intentions.

- It is important because I want to know whether what I am doing is having the sort of beneficial effects I had hoped.

- It is important because I want to know whether what I am being advised to do is helping me to improve the learning in my classroom.

- Researching my practice in this way is important because this is what I think it means to be a professional educator.

Your reasons and the meanings you give to the words may well be different. You will tax your own philosophical thinking in coming to a better understanding of yourself.

You might find that saying out loud to yourself why time to reflect and create your research story is important helps you to become clearer in your own understanding. It might sound odd and it might not work for you but it has worked for Marie. The first time she tried it, in the privacy of the car in a traffic jam, she found she couldn't string two words together. Persisting and tolerating the feelings of inadequacy and confusion which she sometimes experiences when learning something very new, she gradually learned to be much clearer for herself. That translated into a confidence communicated when she talked to other people about what she was doing.

Working with others is helpful, cognitively and emotionally. You might want to think about establishing a regular session with a small band of fellow researchers where you feel a commitment to sharing and improving your work with them. That can both be energising and help to keep your thinking time on your list of priorities. You might find a group of fellow enthusiasts exists in school, locally in person or by Internet communication.

Working with your pupils as co-researchers can also be an opportunity that you and they might relish. Joy found this when she worked with her Year 2 pupils. If the children do not want to start their own research story they may jump at the chance to help you with yours. Children can be very stern and insistent taskmasters. Marie ran a course many years ago where a teacher, Mrs Gold, set herself an initial challenge of having a red pen to hand for marking. She shared her goal with her six-year-old pupils and asked them to help her achieve it, a very unusual and bold step in those days. At the next meeting she reported back. The first few days the children reminded her with enthusiasm of her aspiration when she hadn't a pen to hand. They were really encouraging when she had her pen ready and would accept none of her many excuses when she didn't. She also talked about her project with them regularly. In those sessions they helped her realise why it might appear trivial but was important, feel more commitment to actually doing what she said she wanted to do, explore what the problem was and come up with some very creative solutions. These included hanging a pen on a string round her neck and having pots of pens stationed round the room. They encouraged her to try one of the imagined solutions, helped her decide how to collect data that would help her know if she was improving and at the end helped her evaluate what difference it had made in class. When she talked this through with the children they did not just talk about how many times she had a pen; they talked about the unexpected changes that she and the children had come to recognise and felt were important, the quality of the educational relationships in the class. They talked about what they felt was important to them and why. Mrs Gold was not just a class teacher of a large class of children with very diverse needs; she also had the duties of a deputy head to squeeze in, but she had a lot of help keeping her thinking time open; her 36 pupils ensured she did.

As we write this book the national plan for teaching to become a Master's profession is being put into practise. The place of research undertaken by teachers in the classroom to inform and improve practice is also being stressed in most strategies emanating from the government. You may raise your need for time outside the classroom to further your inquiry as an opportunity for the school to support your continuing professional development.

There is an increasing focus on the importance of hearing the voice of learners in learning and developing curriculum and educational contexts that are real and relevant. The primary strategy was launched under the title of Excellence and Enjoyment. Developing practice in this way contributes to realising the Every Child Matters (ECM) agenda, the inclusion agenda, personalisation of learning, assessment for learning and many other strategies and agendas for which time is sometimes made available. There is more support and opportunity for teachers to influence the direction of education than ever before. These can be opportunities to get the time and support to research in this way. Sometimes creative thinking is needed, but as one of Joy's ten-year-old pupils said, 'Nothing is impossible to a child with imagination.' We might echo that nothing is impossible to an educator with imagination, determination and a love of education and children.

Getting Started

Where to start? Start where you are. Some people read something in a book, or hear ideas at a workshop that start their journey. For others it is a moment in the classroom that provides the spark. What helps people prevent it from being a single spark left to fade away or a good idea that never develops, is to write their reflections on what it is that has stimulated them. It might be a scribbled note in a journal, it might be a blog. It might be an email to a friend. Some record is needed.

Sometimes things seem to come together in the most surprising way when you are open to opportunities. This is what happened for Claire Formby, a teacher participating in the Master's programme. She shows how young children can describe their values with amazing clarity, and how her own values influence what she does as she deals with the realities of being an English classroom teacher.

I've been feeling a need for pattern and structure during the past few weeks, caught up as I am in the drudgery of testing, marking, paperwork, organising supply teachers' work and trying to keep up too with other work with the children. I've just been taking one day at a time, not looking too far ahead because the workload has seemed frighteningly large. There are still assemblies to organise, meetings to have, CPD to attend, a major behaviour issue to deal with and end of year reports to hand in!

So it is true to say that I've been feeling a bit sorry for myself, moaning and grumbling my way through most days at school, and at home too.

I do not consciously look for connectedness but I recognise it immediately and am restored by it. This afternoon during a Circle Time on the theme of what friendship meant to the children, one little girl, Catherine, asked if she could have more time to think, 'Because I know what I want to say but I am trying to think of a better way to say it.' A few minutes later she put her hand up and said she had thought about it. Her words were: 'Friendship is showing someone your heart.'

What powerful, image-laden words to describe friendship. I felt like the learner as Catherine explained to all of us that first she had been thinking that friendship was about liking someone very much but those words weren't enough to explain what she wanted to say. Even now, hours later and writing about this, I can feel the emotion in her words and my response to them. The words make a meaning that I can understand and connect with. Catherine has reminded me about what really matters to me in my vocation and it has put everything else into perspective again!'

If you never go any further with creating your educational research story than to make a note, we would urge you to do so. Such moments are easily missed or forgotten in the rush of life. Writing gives you an opportunity to savour and enjoy them and appreciate the importance of the quality of educational practise you value. Imagine reading a note, such as Claire wrote, years later. How would you feel? So keeping a journal can be a source of pleasure to you and if you are generous enough to share such moments, as Claire did, then you can bring that pleasure to others. Claire's story didn't just brighten Marie's day when she read it, it brightened the day for a lot of other educators who read it subsequently. We hope you are amongst them.

Not all your moments are recognised at the time as earth moving. Sometimes you may start with odd notes, just a few lines scribbled down about something that at the time may have seemed unimportant, mundane, unpleasant… Reflecting on them, sometimes years later, you may see things in a different light, as happened for Ros.

As technology becomes easier to use then you might find photographs and video become part of your journal. Joy had a camera always handy in her classroom for children as well as herself to use and took this photograph.

Toby and Lara hug

'For me this photograph sums up the ethos and educational responsibility that I feel is so important in my classroom. Here two children are genuinely sharing a moment of success after persevering to solve a problem together. The pleasure shines from Toby's face and they hug, as others smile and share their joy. All children should have the inner strength to take risks, to question the world around them and feel a sense of responsibility and success through their learning.'

Some people have a question they want to pursue and launch straight into an explicit action reflection cycle. Others might start with writing about what was really important to them in their life that shaped what they wanted to do or influenced them to want to be a teacher. Wherever you start is the right place for you.

Another Step

As your documentation accumulates, make notes of moments you recognise of importance, odd meanderings, reflections, imagined possibilities, a quote or an incident. If your collection includes photos, videos, emails and so on, make a note of the date and the context and keep a copy of any permissions you have in writing. From significant reading keep a note of author, date, title, publisher/journal. You will come to a point when you need to move to the systematic phase of your research.

Look at what you have collected. You may find it helpful to use a framework to organise the material. We have used our own versions of TASC or an action planner.

1) What do I want to improve?

2) Why do I feel that something could be improved in what I am doing? (This is concerned with what really matters to me in terms of the values that give meaning and purpose in my life. These are the explanatory principles that explain why I do what I do.)

3) What could I do that might improve what I am doing? (Imagining possibilities and choosing one of them to act on in an action plan)

4) As I am progressing what data will I collect to enable me to judge my educational influence in my professional context?

5) As I evaluate the educational influences of my actions in my own learning and the learning of others, who might be willing to help me to strengthen the validity of my explanation of my learning with responses to questions such as:

  i) Is my explanation as comprehensible as it could be?

  ii) Could I improve the evidential basis of my claims to know what I am doing?

  iii) Does my explanation include an awareness of historical and cultural influences in what I am doing and draw on the most advanced social theories of the day?

  iv) Am I showing that I am committed to the values that I claim to be living by?

6) In the light of the evaluation the concerns, action plans and actions are often modified and the process of improvement and Educational knowledge-creation continues.

As you organise and reorganise your thinking write. Don't just leave the thoughts in your head. Use pictures, photographs and video clips to help to show what you are meaning. Describe why a picture or video clip is important to you, what it is it that you are seeing that is significant even if at first you can't explain clearly. This is the first step to creating a living educational theory research account. Creating a living theory account often goes through two phases.

Phase 1

First you write to understand for yourself and as you write you reflect in a different way than when you are 'in the moment'. It may sound strange but it helps you listen to yourself with far more care than when your thinking is left in your head. You discover things about what you are doing that you didn't realise before. Sometimes you find you are doing something you really value, sometimes you find you are doing almost the opposite of what you intended. You become clearer about what you are doing in your practice and what you think is important. It is hard work. As adults we are rarely expected to think, applying those creative and philosophical thinking skills we want our pupils to learn. We can empathise with our pupils when they seem to just want to be told what to do, resist thinking for themselves and don't want to take responsibility for their learning. We have to walk our own talk and can find learning is as scary, exciting, exhilarating, difficult and hard work as it is for our pupils! The first complete draft of a living theory account becomes a situation in which you are clarifying your meanings in the course of the writing itself. When you read this complete, first draft you will often be excited by the endings as this is where clarity emerges about the values and understandings that give meaning and purpose to your life in education and the question that you have been addressing. This comes as a surprise to many.

Phase 2

This first draft then needs transforming into an account that will communicate to other people. It is strange to find that in redrafting with an audience in mind you really begin to understand what you are about. The introduction describes the question, the meanings that have emerged towards the end of your initial draft and helps the reader know how the writings are organised, to enable them to understand your response to your question. It is a bit like a detective story that sets out the clues, investigates and tests, and finally finds the answer. As you write you will want to include the ideas of other people which helped you form your question and develop your inquiry. Sometimes these are ideas that you have integrated, sometimes you will want to say why you didn't use them.

In creating your accounts of your own living educational theories you will come to recognise and value yourself as a knowledge-creator who is creating your own explanations for your educational influences in learning. This will enhance the learning of the other members of the profession if you are generous enough to offer them to others.

Where to Next?

As teachers we take many roles in relation to our pupils, such as instructor, trainer, mentor, leading learner… but in these educational research stories we focus on our primary purpose as educators, that is, to have an educational influence on the learning of our pupils. In these stories we focus on describing, understanding and explaining the educational improvements we are making. Jack Whitehead (2008) clarifies what we mean, '…educational improvements that concern the improvement of life – not simply skill.' Jack Whitehead originated Living Educational Theory (Whitehead, 1989, Whitehead and McNiff, 2006) and that is what we have been using to guide our own research to improve what we are doing.

The phrase 'Educational influences in learning' may be unfamiliar to you, but we like it as it says more about what as educators we are trying to do. Something that suggests a simplistic cause and effect relationship between what we do and our pupils' learning is to misrepresent and misunderstand the complexity of influences that culminate in what, how and why people learn, not simply a skill but to live a life they feel is satisfying and productive.

'Creating their own explanations…' may also be an unfamiliar phrase. It means an individual describes what they are doing and offers an explanation, a theory, to explain why they do what they do and why they have this or that educational influence. The 'Why?' is not, 'Because I was told to.' The 'Why?' is in terms of my educational values. For instance, Marie expresses her living educational values as a loving recognition, a respectful connectedness and an educational responsibility towards others. She can describe her practice and with these principles give an explanation as to why she does what she does, with evidence to show what she means by the living theory of her practice and the standards by which she judges improvement. Marie likes the use of the word 'living' as she feels her values, theory and practice are both what she is living, her embodied knowledge expressed, and they are living, evolving in dynamic multidimensional relationships within and between people and herself, growing and fed by her experiences of life. There are many examples of living theory accounts created by educators on Jack Whitehead's website http://www.actionresearch.net, which is a good place to start if you want to learn to develop your practice through educational research.

By making explicit, offering and testing our own theories we are developing ourselves as creative professional educators, able to substantiate our claim to know what we are doing, able to make rational, logical and reasonable decisions as to the best course of action we should take to improve the educational experience of the children we have an educational responsibility towards. We often find out what our values and theories are, and think creatively about how we might live them more fully, by looking at what we are actually doing in practice already. Creating a living theory account is part of that research process often taking our thinking to places previously unreached, and becomes embedded in our everyday practice. It is not something done 'after the event' just to give a historical report, it embraces the creative process of communicating to and with others and ourselves as a transformational systematic phase of educational research. It takes us to places we would not be able to get to if we just stayed 'in the moment' and our reflections and thinking was always 'in our heads'. The writing and creating of the account through the systematic phase of the research is hard and hence we tend to avoid it. Professor Moira Laidlaw told Marie what her teacher had said to her many years ago. 'Moira, it's not just the number of words, you know. It's the quality of them and if they are arranged in the right order. So many chances of getting it wrong!' How right she was! We must overcome our fear of 'getting it wrong', if our pupils and we are to learn.

We still believe the only people who can learn are the learners themselves and we are in a better position to help our pupils learn by actively exploring our own learning and researching, alongside them.

Chapter 11

Where We Are and What We Have Learned

This book has been a long time in gestation and creation. Through writing together our thinking has been informed and has moved on. We have also been responding to other demands and opportunities, which have added to the mix. So from triumphs and disasters and the quiet space in between we have walked our own talk and continued to research our practice, tried to describe and explain, to improve with the creative and philosophical thinking we have offered as useful tools for the classroom.

We wanted to conclude this book with our stories of our thinking, the ones we have been creating since Chapter 2. They are still ongoing but this is a place to pause for breath and reflect. We wanted to show you that these stories do not start with simple questions, and don't have neat endings where the grail of the fanciful perfect educator sits. Education is a delight for us because it is forever developing and we can influence it by what we do and think. We are different, it is what we understand by learning. Our pupils are different and the times we live in have never been experienced before. If some of what we say seems unfathomable then that is probably because we are still trying to understand. We do hope that some of what we say communicates and either causes you to challenge assumptions in your practice or nudges a thought, which stimulates you to imagine possibilities as to how you might improve the quality of education for yourself and your pupils. At least it helps to know you are not alone in wanting to bring creative and philosophical thinking into the classroom with pleasure and passion.

Ros's Evolving Story

I'd like to invite you into a very private viewing of how and possibly why my interest in creative thinking and philosophy developed. It is the story that accompanies what I began, and continue to do in the classroom, but this story is based on what was going on inside me.

Writing this has been a severe challenge for me. I enjoy writing and have kept personal journals and written stories for years. The physical process of putting words on paper isn't a problem for me. At least I didn't think it was until the suggestion for this book became more than just an idea. Putting down in words what I have done and why over a period of years has been a stressful experience. Not because I don't believe personally in the value of what I do, but because it's very central to the person I am and that requires me to bare my soul to the readers with the possibility that they will find fault with my motives or values, the very things that define me as the person I am. Like many teachers I have this idea that somewhere out there is the 'perfect' way to teach and if I refine and adapt what I do, eventually I will achieve it.

It's rather like a quest for the Holy Grail and just as elusive. If I continue teaching for another ten years till retirement age, with over thirty years of classroom experience behind me, I still doubt whether that chalice will be in my possession. And yet I accept this as being part of what I do. Only when every pupil is motivated to learn and exceeding all expectations will I think that I've done a reasonable job. There is always room for improvement. This again I realise is part of who I am, part of my life values. Whatever I do today I can improve on tomorrow.

The two main questions I want to explore here are why I began on the road of creative thinking and philosophy and what I have personally learned from explaining what I have done to a wider audience. The two are very closely linked and at times I can't distinguish between cause and effect. The common thread between them is me and this is why the boundaries are so difficult to define. What I do is tied in with who I am, the life values

I hold and my own experiences. But experience is never a static thing. We may initially act in one way because of previous incidents, but that produces a new set of experiences and we move on again.

Confession time! I never really intended to go into teaching. There was no blinding light on my road to Damascus with a voice telling me this was my purpose in life. I had very little experience of children and I certainly liked life to be orderly and calm. Mediocre A level results changed all that and so I ended up at teacher training college, preparing to teach German and primary children, a combination which went out of fashion before the course was finished. Many years later I'm still in the classroom by choice, with still a part of me wondering if I should be there!

My own explanation for why I continue to teach is linked to the fact that it is a job that is never the same two days running, let alone two years. Grumble though I might about the 20 years of new strategies and frameworks, there is always a sense of moving on to something better and more effective. The grass never grows under your feet. No year group of children is identical to the last. I may have spent the last 20 years at the same school, but it has never been a repetitive experience and there's still a sense of freshness and challenge about it. I can be creative, change the way I do things, work with new ideas and have a certain amount of autonomy in how I do things. I wonder how many other occupations can make that claim.

There are two 'whys' to answer. One is why I began and the other is why I continue. Following the road of creative thinking and philosophy was probably a natural development for me. It's hard to identify where it all began and the why continues to elude me. There are lots of things that have become more understandable with hindsight but I'm still wrestling with trying to identify what in particular made this something I wanted to pursue. I could have opted for an easier life, just followed the official guidelines on teaching and made sure that I delivered lessons with pace and challenge that were suited to the children's abilities and covered the learning objectives. I would have fulfilled my requirements as a teacher and all would be fine. So why have I opted for extending what I do beyond the basic requirements?

Initially I think I'd probably reached a stage in my career where I'd more or less mastered the basics of the job. You begin by conscientiously following all the guidance you received at college until the raw newness wears off and a confidence in knowing how to do things takes its place. Then comes a time when you gain other bits of experience and probably feel quite secure about what you do. But teaching has a more relational quality about it in that when the honeymoon period is over you begin to wonder if there shouldn't be more to life than this. Not in terms maybe of workload or initiatives, but in the underlying purpose of what you are trying to achieve, the values of what you do. The initial excitement fades into routine and for me it brought a certain jadedness that made me want to regain some of the energy I'd felt in the past.

Life has that way of throwing something in your direction when you need it, whether you have realised the need or not. At every stage in my life, whenever there has been an empty lull something has cropped up to fill it. Happy coincidence maybe, but I feel the opportunities are always out there, only we're not looking. A combination of events began a new episode for me professionally. My head at that time was new to the school and very keen to get us motivated and extending ourselves. She herself was interested in opening new horizons up for our children, helping them to see that the world was theirs for the taking if they wanted. She had already made links with the APEX programme locally, set up by Marie, for more able pupils. It was at her suggestion that we attended a twilight session on Bloom's Taxonomy and courses on extending pupils.

She gave me the responsibility in school for Gifted and Talented education, then very much in its infancy, and thoroughly supported the idea of giving our children a chance to experience a broader curriculum. It didn't matter that they didn't own a packet of crayons or a sketchbook. They were packed off with supplies from the stock cupboard, taken there if needed. Golden clubs, run by the children themselves, and activity weeks became part of school life and invigorated the atmosphere of the school. There was something about these experiences that had energy of its own. The children loved them, the adults found them more relaxing than 'teaching' and I was fascinated by the change in the way the children approached what they were doing. I now think of this in terms of a power shift between teacher as director and co-learning with the children, an area still to examine further in greater depth.

It wasn't long after all this began that I met Marie at my local gym and agreed to help out at an APEX workshop. The rest is history. Involvement with APEX workshops and summer schools has been a source of great pleasure and personal learning ever since and helped me broaden my idea of what educating a child should be about. They have also been instrumental in my own development as a learner and helped establish my understanding that I enjoy extending myself as a learner.

I am indebted to the head, Kate St John, sadly no longer with us. She gave me a challenge that she thought me capable of, recognising a talent in me that I had not seen myself. I feel she would be proud of what I've done with it and recognise the tribute I am paying to her perception. Although I didn't see it in these terms at the time, I've come to see that this is what I strive to do with the children I teach. I'm not just there to fill their heads with information, my chosen role is looking to find a glimmer of something they are good at, but maybe don't realise yet themselves.

It was not just that someone had recognised a potential in me that kept me going, but rather it was finding I had a genuine love for the creative and sometimes quirky in life. Discussing philosophical issues and thinking 'outside the box' appeals to me and gives me great pleasure. When that question came about plants getting fat I was already predisposed to find it interesting. It rekindled the type of conversations I used to have with my father, who was equally a lateral thinker, much, I suspect, to the exasperation of my mother.

So to answer the 'why' of beginning creative thinking and philosophy is to acknowledge that I was ready for something different and wanted a greater excitement from learning than the standard curriculum provided or inspired me to do. In being ready for this I was therefore able to tune in to an opportunity when it arose. If I hadn't felt a bit bored or jaded with routine then I would have ignored the chance and any unusual question or professional development opportunity offered to me by Kate or Marie would have been missed.

The reasons as to why I have continued are like a patchwork of pieces of cloth. The patterns or colours go well together, providing an overall theme, but the links have not appeared until the patchwork has grown. I love the sense of novelty I get from these sessions and even more, I love the enthusiasm they produce in the children. Only recently we had a class SEAL lesson on changes and I asked the children what they would do differently if they were in charge of a school like ours. There were some very practical suggestions, like changing the sports facilities or extending playtimes. The response that interested me most was being told they would like to have some choice in what they learned, particularly the afternoon lessons, and that they would like more 'fun' lessons. When I asked if they could give me an example of this, the reply was that they liked using their imaginations and that the lesson about aliens had been great. This was a last minute creative session that had been astoundingly successful in producing enthusiasm and generating ideas, I had enjoyed it, so had they, and it was one of those times when I could work alongside them instead of having to control them.

One of the things I am coming to see more clearly as a driving force behind the things I do is myself as a learner. Each day brings some increasing awareness of how the way I learn compares to how others learn. The two are closely interlinked. It doesn't matter if the person facing the new learning experience is a child or an adult. Both encourage me to put myself in their shoes and try to understand how I would approach the same issue, what strategies I would use, how my approach can be useful to them or their approach useful to me. For some this might seem a little too introspective, but I have found it very helpful to have a heightened awareness of how I learn in order to help others learn or deal with problems.

Backed up by many of the books I have read on learning, intelligence and education, I have come to my own theories of learning. Sometimes the reading has reinforced and made comprehensible aspects that I have come to be aware of on my own. At other times it has helped me understand what I could do and given me suggestions for changes. None of it is a one-size fits all solution that comes readymade and instantly applicable. Every person has their own style of learning and working, and these are not fixed but rather there is a fluidity of moving from one to another depending on the situation and circumstances.

Despite all of us having preferred ways of learning which might be lumped together in rough areas there are other factors which override anything else. These are the ones that I try to pass on in my professional life, the ones that are more important to me than whether the child is a visual, auditory or kinaesthetic learner. It goes beyond trying to identify any of Howard Gardner's learning types, even though awareness of these is useful in adapting the way we teach.

My theories of learning, and what education should be about, come from my own experiences and reflections as child, school, student, adult learner and teacher. They may be totally different to other people's and yet I feel there is something universal in the conclusions I have reached.

The most important key to learning successfully is to have an inner desire to learn. It has to be something you really want to do, whatever your motives for wanting to do it. As young children we are learning all the time, regardless of whether it is something that adults want us to learn. There is a curiosity and a satisfaction about it, a certain energy that drives us. It is this energy and enthusiasm that seems to wane when formal education takes over. We can learn under other conditions such as the fear of failure or the desire to obtain a certain type of employment, but this learning, while it may finally lead to a pleasure in itself, is often a chore and something we leave behind as soon as we can.

I think I must have always had that inner love of learning, but at some point I ceased to be taught the things I really wanted to learn about and became sidetracked into thinking that school curriculums and college courses were the main source of information. While the education system strives to provide the individual with a general outline of knowledge, the structure can be very rigid and directive. Despite changes, much of the content of the curriculum, or the way it is approached, remains very similar to my schooling, and probably that of at least one generation before me. Aptitudes are looked for within a restrictive range of subjects and as you progress through the system the choices get smaller. I am not alone in having to 'give up' certain subjects at secondary school because I was better at others and exam results were important.

My personal response seems to have been to separate 'real learning', the stuff you did at school with a practical end view, from 'hobbies and interests' which are things you pursue for pleasure. There were many things that I did not take seriously as learning, and also many areas that I avoided on the assumption that as I had no qualifications in them then I could not be any good at them. Over the years, however, I have come to realise that there are many skills and bits of knowledge that I have built up through my own efforts in which I have a greater degree of confidence and ability than many of the subjects I studied formally. Mathematics, beyond basic arithmetic, was forever a source of anxiety and confusion to me, and yet now I have a greater understanding through teaching it because I have made the concepts understandable to myself by working through them towards personal understanding.

What I find has happened through my journey in creative and philosophical thinking is that a love of learning for itself has been rekindled. It is not confined to a syllabus or curriculum objective. It enjoys that delicious freedom of being complete in itself; an expansion of my own learning in its widest sense. If for no other reason than this I shall continue to develop my interest in the curious and thought-provoking, in the hope that future generations and other teachers will join in the fun.

Joy's Evolving Story

'The time is now, break free and fly... if you have the courage!'

This was how my opening story ended, a temptation to other teachers to take a risk, feel the freedom and energy that can be co-created by trying creative and philosophical thinking in their classrooms. But as I have written this book, often struggling to explain ideas and feelings, the meaning is also for me.

Writing has always felt soothing. I don't find it easy to share my thoughts aloud, push forward an opinion or challenge thinking, but on paper the words flow, forming my tale in a fluid, poetic form. The combination of the words and 'feel' is equally as important as the content I am trying to share. If I am honest I write for myself, not the reader, but to clarify and sort my reflections for myself. I write as the journey unfolds, clear to me but a challenge for others as often the clarity of my learning only comes together at the end.

Writing this has for the first time made me aware of my story and I ask myself, what is at the heart of my learning? What has had the most impact and how can I share that with others in a helpful way?

Often my story feels tangled and messy, different strands that sometimes run parallel, sometimes veer away from each other and at others merge together. Often I find myself rambling, ideas springing forth, but not in a clear and logical manner. Writing it down coherently has proved a real challenge, far more difficult than living the journey in the moment.

My perspective has changed in the last year, since I have taken up my first post as a headteacher in Somerset. This has happened at the same time as the three of us began to think about the idea of writing a book about our different and yet similar journeys. Writing has helped me to understand the role I played in my classroom and the children's learning in my care, the strength of the relationships we formed and the co-learning that transformed the ethos and belief of the children and me.

My own story has developed over many years, more than I care to name, but to condense and identify the key themes and moments that enlightened, frustrated and helped my development as a learner and those of the children, as well as our understandings of ourselves, has proved fascinating and frustrating. Many weekends have found the three of us, Marie, Ros and me, huddled over coffee discussing and retelling important moments, ideas, comments from the children and tales of people we have met. It is through this retelling that the light of enthusiasm and passion for learning and connecting with others shines through. It is clear in the body language and facial expressions even if you do not hear the words. It is that sense of sharing, 'connectiveness' that re-energises and sparks new ideas and has helped keep me going when timetables and other pressures seem to be closing in. It is almost therapeutic, charging the battery and something I miss if we do not meet. For me the fun and excitement of real learning comes from this safe environment of critical friendship. Yes we question, but only to strengthen our perspectives or suggest an alternative or complementary path.

This book, almost a diary, feels very personal. Through this retelling, I have had to explore myself, my values and really look critically at my role in the classroom. It feels as though I am opening something of myself to be viewed and challenged by the world. We have discovered no secret formula for learning, but really feel that we have made an important discovery 'for' and 'about' ourselves. I have felt free. Creative. Closer to the teacher I believe I want to be. I want the children to challenge and question the world around them, not only answering my questions, but the tough, unsettling kind that can push the boundaries and make us feel a little uneasy.

For the first time I find myself having to clarify my journey for this book but also for the parents, children, governors and staff in my new school.

The first assignment I wrote as part of my Masters degree at Bath University explored my own 'living values' as a teacher. Dare I confess that this was something I had never had to articulate before, let alone consider and identify? Didn't I fit in with the ethos of the school I worked in and reflect their values? Did I have my own and could they exist if they were different from those around me?

Perhaps the truth of my learning is that I am now comfortable asking myself those uncomfortable questions, those we aren't always aware we should or could ask! I still often have no answers. Definitely not quick, simple answers, but I do enjoy the fact that I have asked them and playing around with them. I feel a sense of confidence and contentment with being different, challenging the format of school life that I have been swamped in.

I have tried journeying alone. At the time I felt the pleasure and passion I had thought I had lost in my teaching, and for a while this brought its own contentment. But I also experienced the frustration of wanting to share it with someone who is like-minded. By like-minded, I only mean someone who wants more. Someone who wants to explore new ideas, someone who is excited, and willing to take a risk in their learning and teaching. For me, and it may not be the same for you, the key has been those lazy discussions we have had together. Those odd moments when I relived a session in my classroom while sharing it with someone else, helped not only me as I was reminded of the pleasure I had felt, but it sorted and deepened my own learning as well as, I hope, that of the others. I have found that I learn a lot at the time, more reflecting afterwards, but the depth, forging and creation of knowledge for me comes from the clarification through sharing it with someone else. At first this was very much through my writing, which was safer, less threatening. The next step was explaining it, being challenged about it. Then I realised the value of feeling the flow of energy and pleasure that is generated by enthusiastic learners, reflecting and sharing together.

This understanding is the core strand that I feel I want to develop in my new school where we share a sense of a learning journey for staff and pupils together. Living theory action research will link all learners in our school. I am excited that this book is nearly finished. I am really excited about the future. Yes I know I am using that word again, but it is the only one that will do. Excited. I am excited because I see the next pathway in my journey, a journey that will link with the learning of others developing new stories and a whole school approach.

Previously I have introduced ideas to the school as part of the management team, after having tested and tried them myself, often, over a long period of time. But now in a new school and county I am faced with a new challenge. Recently I attended a meeting in Bath, where articulate sixth formers presented their research using the TASC Wheel by Belle Wallace. Another headteacher of a large primary school asked how he could sort all of the ideas about learning, the curriculum, timetabling, and management into a form that he could introduce in his school. Something that is manageable but means we are not all struggling with similar mistakes and developmental processes in our schools. This is a question that has been troubling me also, and has run around my mind through the course of writing this book.

The timing of this book has coincided with my first few months at my new school. It has given me a break from experimenting with ideas and researching in my classroom. Instead as I have been 'finding my feet' I have been sharing, reflecting and discussing my experiences, helping me to clarify and think about introducing creative, reflective learning in my new school.

From the past I have looked for ways of developing the 'voice' of the pupils in my class, their confidence as learners but also belief and understanding of themselves. As headteacher I have also been exploring how that can be incorporated into our vision for the school and feed clearly through the 'paperwork' linking to our school development plan, performance management, school council and in fact every aspect of school life.

At present no student body has access to a platform to share their learning and views or to question developments and the direction of schools. It is only very recently that pupils are being asked to help develop and inform policy. Adults are just beginning to consult children about the management of schools and the delivery of the curriculum, how they learn but not what they learn. Their abilities as knowledge creators are not recognised or valued. The children I have worked with feel strongly that often grown ups like children and want to help them, but don't talk to and listen to children enough and have forgotten what it is like to be a child.

'Why don't they ask us?' Beth complained. I hesitate to answer, 'I don't know why!' Is it because we never have asked the children, because we teach them and they learn? Does it stem from the old adage that children should be seen and not heard? Or do we feel we know better as the adults? Perhaps another option could answer, 'Because it has always been this way....'

The journey we have shared has been unsettling, but I feel for the first time that perhaps blinkers have been removed and there is a whole world outside the 'box' that I have accepted, that I was not even aware of before the journey we shared. Approaches to action research like the ones we have experimented with can provide a link between learners, forming cycles of reflective learning and questions that together we can explore. The change in relationships, when open, shared learning happens in the classroom, is fascinating and liberating.

I feel confident in the future. A future in which, if we are brave enough, we can try new ways of learning and creating knowledge for ourselves. For the first time in many years we have the imagination and ability to change, we have the justification from the strategies to take a risk, to look to the future and develop a culture of 'I can' and 'I wonder…' in our schools. A school ethos of shared mentoring and learning, led by all, connected and confident in themselves, their lives and relationships. Co-existing and co-creating knowledge and wisdom through life as Gert Beista (2006) says, 'We might look at learning as a response to what is other and different, to what challenges, irritates, or even disturbs us, rather than as the acquisition of something we want to possess.'

We begin and end as a circle, and in a cycle of questions and uncertainty that we don't always have a definitive answer to. But that is the glory of the journey. It is the end of this moment but just transient in our life of learning.

Marie's Evolving Story

I am reflecting back over what I wrote in Chapter 2 and the story I wrote, which finished:

> 'I work from the premise that all children and young people hold within themselves the possibility of living a satisfying and productive life and the ability to make a valued and valuable contribution to their own lives and the lives of us all. I believe there is no predetermined limit as to what that contribution might be. I do not mean that I believe children are able to grow up to achieve anything they might choose, rather I believe it is not possible to predict what they might achieve during their lifetime through the combination of opportunity and their determined inclination and commitment to realising their aspirations. My purpose as an educator is to open the imaginations of children and young people to the various possibilities of them living their lives in ways they find satisfying and productive and enable them to develop the confidence and competences to make and act on informed decisions as to what they want to do as they enter the adult world.

> I believe the individual is the only one who can determine whether her life is satisfying and productive, and she does so according to her own living values as standards by which to make such judgments.

> And that is where I am now, trying to walk my own talk and learn from trying to understand and improve my own theories to explain what I do, contributing to improving the educational experience of children and young people.'

This still works for me. I have had a moment of revelation recently as to what my values are that explain and inform what I do in practice, my living theory of my practice, and which form the basis from which I judge the standard of my work. It might sound odd to you when I admit that I have just begun to understand my values and my living theory, but I think I am not alone and many people often don't really know what they are doing, and that is not just in education. The result is we are in a poor position to improve our practice and in no position to respond to the demands of others, for instance the government, professionally.

I think to ask the question, 'How do I improve my educational practice?' makes the implicit assumptions that I know what my educational practice is and can give a reasoned and reasonable account of what I do and the educational standards by which I evaluate it. For me that is the beauty of living theory research, there is an overt recognition that as an educator my values are my bedrock of researching my practice, and emerge through examining what I do. My theories are living in the sense that I am living them and living in the sense that they are forever evolving in a complex context, which includes me, other people, society and the world. Understandings of living theory are also living, so I suggest you visit the http://www.actionresearch.net website and explore online, in print and in conversations to see if the learning stories of other people inspire and contribute to your own journey.

These are the values that are core to me, which enable me to explain why I do what I do and which enable me to hold myself accountable:

- A loving recognition.

- A respectful connectedness.

- An educational responsibility towards…

I, like you, have constraints and targets but these three phrases mean something real to me when I think about the quality of education and what I might do to improve my contribution. When I look back over the stories we have given you in this book I can see these qualities expressed. It is how I understand what a good educator does and what happens in an educational space and in educational relationships. I would prefer to be able to show you what I mean but will have to be content here to try to communicate through text and ask you to use your imagination to think of when you have experienced these qualities yourself as educator and student.

Loving Recognition

What do I mean? I mean recognising the person within, not just the shell but beyond to the possibilities that person may not see of themselves but would value if they did. Gert Biesta (2006) talked about the need for a language of education, and not just learning, and in that context bringing into presence that unique 'I', which I understood him to mean what it is that only I can say or offer, when 'I' is not replaceable by anyone else.

We spend a lot of time telling children what they will become, their potential, what destiny that is set for them and so concern ourselves with 'underachievement' and teaching children to become 'better' learners according to some disembodied standard. It concerns me that we then seem to lose sight of the very special and unique person within, the person who is more than 'a learner', 'a pupil', a label of one form or another.

I recognise the importance of stimulating and exciting children to explore and develop the confidence, skills and sophistication as knowledge creators. But somehow there must be a way of providing that in schools in a way that enhances the child's recognition and valuing of themselves and their unique contributions to their own wellbeing and that of others. Categorising children and labelling them seems to repeat and amplify the error.

I know when I experience a good educator. They offer me a loving recognition; the very personal me inside that is trying, with the best of intent, to be the best I can be and feels recognised; sometimes they offer me an insight into who I am and can be that I do not see or understand myself.

This is what I see in Barry Hymer's (2007) story that he gave at the beginning of his thesis:

In 2002 my book on gifted and talented learners was published (Hymer & Michel, 2002). It opened with a reflection on my last year of full-time teaching, and in particular my memory of an incident involving a Year 5 (ten-year-old) boy, known as Robert in the book:

Robert was a large boy, considered something of a bully by other children and he was challenging in the classroom. He had moderate generalised learning difficulties and he was functionally illiterate. And a few weeks before the end of the school year, I also discovered he was gifted. Not globally gifted, not outrageously or psychometrically gifted, but still gifted. I discovered his gift by accident. Our school had been participating in the W H Smiths 'Poets in Schools' scheme, which had brought the poet David Orme ('Mango Chutney') to work with students across the entire Year 5 year-group. As one of their poetry-writing exercises, the children had gone out in small groups to explore – in great and close detail – the trees and shrubs adjoining the school's playing fields. They'd reflected, taken notes, drawn observational sketches, seen the trees and leaves and insects in new lights and from new angles, played with language, laughed and had fun. And then they'd returned to the classroom to knock their thoughts, notes, perceptions and reflections into poems. I'd been with Robert and his group throughout their time outside – mostly to manage his tendency to distract others – but back in the classroom my attention was shared with other members of the class. By the time I got around to Robert's desk, he'd managed an illegible sentence, in his typically tight, misspelled and dysfluent script. I asked him what he'd written and there was a long pause as he tried to make sense of his work. Then he replied, in a voice so slow and soft I hardly heard him: 'Even the winter leaves have their own secret colours.'

That was it. One line. But what a line! It was mid-summer, and Robert had found and studied a solitary, decaying winter-leaf. And in his observations and his slow reflections, Robert captured an image that contained a most deliberate metaphor. He was saying, I'm convinced, 'Mr Hymer, notice me. I know I've not got a great deal going for me in school, but just sometimes, in some situations, I can do things that will amaze you'. The children's best efforts were collated and published in-house in an anthology entitled, 'Their Own Secret Colours'. With the support of David Orme, Robert introduced the anthology to the parents at the official 'launch'. He later told me it was the first time he'd ever been asked to do something important. Robert's moment in the sun coincided with a staggering change in his attitude and performance in school. He saw himself as a poet, as someone who – under the right conditions – could amaze with the power of his words. He still struggled to read and write and acquire new concepts at the speed of his classmates but the bullying pretty much stopped, the friendships and peer-respect grew, and Robert walked around the school and playgrounds with a real, deep and growing sense of self-confidence. He seemed caught up in a virtuous circle. And if that was the effect of Robert's self-perception, who was I to disillusion him? A few weeks later the term and school year ended. I left the school and the area and I've no idea what became of him.

I think it was what Mitch Albom (1997) was getting at when he described the influence of Morrie Schwartz, his college tutor:

'I came to love the way Morrie lit up when I entered the room. He did this for many people, I know, but it was his unique special talent to make each visitor feel that the smile was unique. "Ahhhh, it's my buddy," he would say when he saw me, in that foggy, high-pitched voice. And it didn't stop with the greeting. When Morrie was with you, he was really with you. He looked you straight in the eye, and he listened as if you were the only person in the world. How much better would people get along if their first encounter each day were like this...?'

I know people who can walk into a room and bring sunshine with them. The teacher as a wonderful educator seems to be able to do this and find the sunshine in each child, and enable that child to enjoy what they have within and find the courage and enthusiasm to help it shine out for themselves and others to benefit from.

Respectful Connectedness

Perhaps if I start with saying what I don't mean this might become clearer. In traditional relationships there is a one-way connection between teacher and pupils with the intention of transmitting information. In 'child centred' classrooms there still seems to be a one-way connection between teacher and pupils, but this time the power of control over the inquiry has shifted to the child, while the teacher serves the function of providing them with information and skills that will enable them to do what it is they are striving to do. This is sometimes described as moving from being 'sage on the stage', to 'guide on the side'. At times these relationships are appropriate, but I would suggest that there is an educational relationship that might be described as a 'respectful connectedness', where there is a recognition and respect for the contribution of skills, information, understanding, personal qualities... that teacher and pupils can make to the learning and inquiry where new knowledge is created. There is also a care and respect for each other's boundaries. These boundaries are living and dynamic and when a teacher offers respectful connectedness they are sensitive to the boundaries of the pupils as well as their own.

This extract by Louise Cripps (2007) illustrates something of what I mean. She and four of her ten-year-old pupils are taking part in a day of collaborative inquiry and she writes:

I really appreciate the flow of focused conversation between us all as we try out different understandings. The conversation also requires the learners to be understanding of each other and their difficulties, and so a reflective quality was built in.

There was no imposition by anyone on the others in the group. I felt that I, as a learner, wasn't pushed or rushed into being able to do something at the expense of really understanding it, and I also felt that the others in the group felt in the same position although we all had different levels of knowledge or understanding about the task.

Throughout the activity at the time, I was very aware of the way in which the knowledge and understanding was being woven throughout us all. This activity couldn't have happened without the relational flow between the learners in the group.

There was a real connection between the four of us as learners as the ideas passed from one to another.

Geraldine starts off with the knowledge, but wants to share it. It was her challenge to help us understand.

Louis very quickly shows that he knows what it was all about, and keeps testing what he sees against the ideas already in his head.

Edward quietly watches, and is given the space to keep working out what is happening. I am aware that at the beginning he is as puzzled as I am, but my perception is that he is seeking clarity in the same way as me. This is reinforced for me by watching the video, when near the beginning we unconsciously mirror the same kind of thinking body language. I am aware with Edward of a breakthrough moment when amidst all the chat, he quietly reaches out and picks up the cards to try something out. At that stage I don't think it quite works out, but I think Edward has found a new theory to pursue.

Also in terms of the dynamic of the group, each respects the other and the learning of the other, and makes space for it. This activity isn't just a polite exchange of ideas, it is real collaboration.

There are separate conversations and exchanges happening throughout as well, but not to the exclusion of others in the group.

I want to know what Louis's understanding is because I am fascinated by what his thinking is, and he is able to articulate it. He wants to know what my thinking is because he wants to understand where I am, so he can show me more clearly how to understand. Although we all know each other, we haven't worked in exactly this way together before, and I'm thinking that it makes explicit the quality of relationship which must exist, and which I greatly value as an educator, but which I wouldn't take for granted.

As I watch the clip, I'm also fascinated about what the other learners bring in terms of their gifts, and I am challenged by the importance of providing opportunities for the learners I am responsible for to develop their gifts.

Louis has really appreciated the chance to work specifically with like-minded people where he knows his ideas will be understood. Although he had developed an understanding very quickly he was happy to wait to explain what he understood. He gave that to the group, and helped us all develop our understanding in an inclusional way.

Geraldine gave us a clear demonstration, and was also very patient in helping us understand, and gave us clear pointers without feeling she had to dominate or be the one who knew. She too was able to read the group and each of us in it, and give us the space we needed.

Edward had the capacity to stay with the task, to listen and watch, and build his understanding in that way.

I feel pleased by my role in the group, as it's how I want to be as an educator. I'm very happy learning alongside others. I want people's ideas to be heard, and I want people to feel valued. I really enjoy engaging with the ideas of others, trying to understand what they're thinking by what they say. Like Louis I find it helpful to know where people are in their thinking and understanding. As an educator if I know that, I can more readily help others move forward in their understanding, and as a learner I can move forward in my own thinking and develop my own understanding.'

It is much easier to understand if you look at the video but I hope this account communicates something that resonates with you. There is a sensitivity that Louis and the children express in their relationships where the connections are channels through which there is a receptive-responsive flow of communication. These are some definitions of the word respect that can be found in the Cambridge on-line dictionary:

- to treat something or someone with kindness and care
- to accept the importance of someone's rights or customs and to do nothing that would harm them or cause them offence.

There is a quality felt in the connectedness, which I describe as respectful; there is a gentle warmth and good humour, good manners, an invitation is extended to offer, accept and co-create which can be declined without rancour, there is a consideration for self and the other, with attention for the wellbeing and well becoming of all, and an optimism of something fruitful which may emerge from the engagement.

The challenge to the educators is how to exercise their judgement, while being non-judgemental about how they bring their pupils into such a relationship. It takes time, skill, determination, courage and self-awareness on behalf of the educators and trust and a willingness to contribute by the pupils. It also requires a recognition that the teachers' boundaries have to be much firmer and more distant with some pupils than others, and the boundaries of some children may be much firmer and more distant than the teacher would like, and remain so.

Educational Responsibility Towards…

If I am expressing an educational responsibility towards others I am acting with their best intent at heart. I will have to do so within the context of the best interests of others but I am focusing on the pupils' best intent. I know this is different to what we usually say, that we work with their best interests at heart. I just wonder how often that means that what it is the pupils are striving for and their voices in their own learning and lives are ignored. I am still wrestling with that.

I think we often feel under pressure to respond to the demands of the institution or organisation for which we work. I remember vividly as a psychologist some years ago working with a girl. She was very capable of getting good grades in her SATs and I was trying to encourage her to do so. Eventually she turned round and told me she had spent a lot of time looking on the Internet for information and had thought about it very carefully. She had come to the conclusion that her SATs grade were of importance to the school for their position in the league tables but they were of no importance to her. She said she and her teachers knew the level of her skills and the quality of her understanding in the curriculum and she would get onto the courses she wanted. She was right. However, it is a very complicated and difficult decision to make as to when it is my educational responsibility to 'push' a child to do something she may not want to do, but which is genuinely in her best interest and will equip her with the confidence and competences necessary for her to realise their best intent. I don't think there is a universally correct answer, but I do believe it is a question that should continually challenge the educator and to which they should be continually checking the appropriateness of their responses in respect to the children in their care.

The distinction I would particularly like to make is between an educational responsibility for and an educational responsibility towards. I don't believe that I can or should take responsibility for anyone apart from myself but I do believe I have a responsibility towards others, by which I mean to help them make and act on decisions that will contribute to their own wellbeing and well-becoming and that of others, and to help them to learn to recognise and keep away from harm.

Developing Forms of Evidence and Accountability

I need to use forms of evidence that communicate the 'humanness', the dynamic and relational nature, of my living values as standards of judgement. This is not just an academic affectation. There are many reasons why I believe it is important that forms of evidence are created that communicate much better the experience of quality education. Evidence should enable us to improve, not just prove, what we do, we get what we look for and in the absence of anything else targets and statistics will continue to be used abusively and inappropriately to evaluate educational quality.

You will have experienced, as I have, the power of static forms of targets and evidence where, despite ourselves, we value what we measure and this is what our practice will be drawn to. The test scores help me decide whether I am on the road or have wandered into the quicksand and they can be useful signposts. But all too often they become destinations, with damaging, unintended consequences. For instance, in our league table culture we work hard to improve a child's reading score and can end up putting them off literature, as a pleasurable form of communication, for life.

I need a form of evidence that communicates the relationally dynamic nature of what I am about. I can describe a loving recognition, a respectful connectedness and an educational responsibility towards another, in text. Some poets and novelists can bring those written words to life with metaphor and other devices, but even so I need more forms to communicate my inclusional values expressed in practice, which can enable me to improve what I am doing and communicate it to other people. Visual images, and particularly video, help considerably to assist the words to reach places otherwise untouched. Pattie Lather (1991) points out that we can never really represent our reality. However, I think creating a visual narrative with video comes closer than text alone.

For a video narrative to communicate I believe I need to work hard to 'decentre', which Victor Quinn (1997) describes well: 'Decentring is a vital idea. It is the achievement whereby I learn what it is that you need to hear or experience in order to share what is in my mind, whether it be a question, an idea or a supportive anecdote.'

He also points out that it is 'very, very hard' and not often broached in school. I will go further and say I don't think it is often broached anywhere else either. Victor Quinn quotes Wood (1997): 'Being relatively inexperienced and lacking expertise in the task of analysing and evaluating their own and other people's verbal communications, most young children assume that failures of communication are necessarily the fault of whoever is listening.'

I would suggest that this trait is not just that of young children and I, like many adults, have to continually be mindful that not being able to communicate clearly may indicate the learning I still need to be engaged with. It is interesting to me to find that in trying to communicate to others more effectively I am improving my communication with myself and have begun to listen more attentively to what I and others are saying, to keep trying to go beyond the words to the feelings and implicit understandings.

So, my story still has more questions than answers but in offering the evidence from the application of the creative and philosophical thinking we have been considering in this book, I think my belief is justified that I am improving my contribution to an educational experience of quality for the children whom my work might influence.

Last Words

Developing the ability of our children and ourselves to think is something we believe we should be doing. Those approaches with a sound theoretical underpinning and explicit pedagogy can be shown to have an educational influence in children's learning and raise standards. However, we think we are being somewhat perverse if we try to suggest that there is a simple panacea which can be applied without the teachers themselves engaging in creative and philosophical thinking. The upside is that actually walking the talk, improving educational practice by being more the educator you want to be, is invigorating for teachers and pupils alike.

We improved what we did with our pupils by going beyond the notion of creative and philosophical thinking as just another fashion to contend with and amending a few lessons here or there. We explored over a long time why we think it important to improve our own creative and philosophical thinking as we encouraged our pupils to improve their creative and philosophical thinking. This leads us to continually explore ideas, examine what we are doing and act, reflect and change the educational contexts we create for and with them in the everyday classroom.

Creating and telling educational research stories of the form we have been talking about takes time, effort, determination and a commitment to learning. Getting them listened to is no less difficult and complex but equally worthwhile. As Jean McNiff (2006) says, 'First, there is the business of what kind of story to tell and how to tell it... Second, there is the business of getting people to listen to the story.' We would add that there is also learning to listen to and value our own story and those of other people.

In writing this book we have been trying to tell some of our own research stories to ourselves and to you. In doing that we have challenged and improved our own learning. We will know if our story has been told well if you find something in this book that stimulates your imagination, provokes your own thinking and you begin to create your own stories and support your children in creating theirs.

We want to leave you with these thoughts of Joy's which she expressed in her Masters account titled 'How can I enhance the educational influence of my pupils in their own learning, that of other pupils, myself and the school?' (Mounter, 2008)

> 'It makes me, for the first time more aware of the impact I have personally on the children, the space I create and the sense of self being so important in my classroom.
>
> I hear so often the research that gives children limited voice about aspects of subject knowledge but not the authority as knowledge creators, co-creating together with teachers and the depth of thinking my children confidently share through the narrative of their journey. I read the special issue of Educational Action Research (Vol. 15, No. 3. September 2007) on pupil voice, but was disappointed at the lack of depth of the research. It doesn't go as far as the research my children have done and doesn't share the co-creation of knowledge and voice of self. It still focuses on the given curriculum and children's level of achievement from the teacher's perspective. I have presented through this essay evidence that the children and I together have gone beyond the research and work presented in this edition.

We are creating knowledge together and contributing to the educational knowledge base. Work is shared nationally and internationally through presentations at conferences, for instance Jack Whitehead's keynote in New York (Whitehead, 2008), and through requests for contributions for publication in America and Britain based on my research (Mounter, 2008). We are making a difference. I truly believe I have rediscovered my own living values. They are not changing daily as I grow and learn, but I feel them deepening and strengthening and I am able to articulate them to myself and to others more clearly and confidently. I feel them through the growing confidence reflected in a smile, the moment a child reflects and shares an understanding of themselves or by inspiring someone else to take a risk and try something new.'

We hope you take courage and fly!

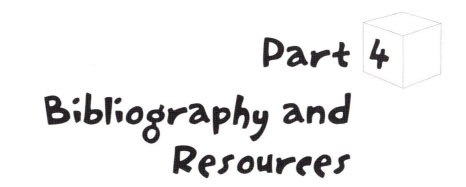

Part 4
Bibliography and Resources

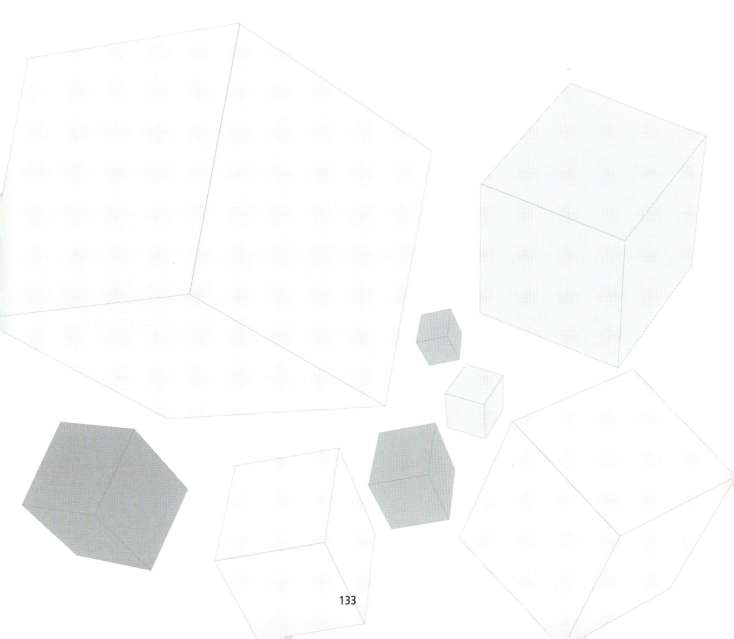

Bibliography

Albom, M. (1997) *Tuesdays with Morrie*. London: Times Warner.

Bassey, M. (1991) 'Creating Education through Research'. *British Educational Research Journal*, Vol.18, No.1, 3-16.

Biesta, G. J. J. (2006) *Beyond Learning: Democratic Education for a Human Future*. Boulder Co.: Paradigm Publishers.

Bloom, B., Englehart, M., Furst, E., Hill, W. & Krathwohl, D. (1956) *Taxonomy of Educational Objectives: The classification of educational goals. Handbook I: Cognitive domain*. New York, Toronto: Longmans, Green.

Brown, J. S. (ed) (1997) *Seeing Differently: Insights on innovation*. Boston, MA: Harvard Business School Publishing.

Cam, P. (1995) *Thinking Together: Philosophical Inquiry for the Classroom*. Sydney: Hale & Iremonger Pty Ltd.

Claxton, G. (2001) *Wise Up*. Stafford: Network Educational Press.

Claxton, G. (2002) *Building Learning Power*. Bristol: TLO Ltd.

Costa, A. L. & Kallick, B. (2000) *Discovering and Exploring Habits of Mind*. USA, VA: Association for Supervision & Curriculum Development.

Covey, S. (1989) *The 7 Habits of Highly Effective People*. London: Simon and Schuster.

Cripps, L. (2007) 'How do I improve my educational relationship with the learners I work with, both adults and children?' *Masters Educational Inquiry*, University of Bath. http://www.jackwhitehead.com/tuesdayma/louiseeenov07.htm [accessed 17th November 2008]

De Bono, E. (1970) *The Dog Exercising Machine*. London: Jonathan Cape.

De Bono, E. (1972) *Children Solve Problems*. London: Penguin Books

De Bono, E. (2007) *How to have Creative Ideas*. Chatham: Vermilion.

Dewey, J. (1916) *Democracy and Education*. New York: Free Press.

DfES (2003) [accessed 22nd September 2008] http://www.standards.dfes.gov.uk/primary/publications/literacy/63553/

DfES (2004) *Every Child Matters: Change for children in schools*. London: Department for Education and Skills.

DfES (2007) '*Module A: Facilitating children and young people's development through mentoring*'. CWDC Induction Training Programme. Learning Mentor Role Specific Modules Practitioner Handbook.

Dweck, C. (2000) *Self-theories: Their role in motivation, personality and development*. Florence, KY: Psychology Press.

Dweck, C. (2006) *Mindset: The new psychology of success*. New York: Random House.

Eisner, E. (1993) 'Forms of Understanding and the Future of Educational Research'. *Educational Researcher*. 22(7), 5-11.

Fisher, R. (1995) *Teaching Children to Think*. Cheltenham: Stanley Thorne Publishers Ltd.

Fisher, R. (2003) *Teaching Thinking.* London: Continuum.

Fisher, R. (2005) *Teaching Children to Think.* Cheltenham: Nelson Thornes.

Fukuyama, F. (1992) *The End of History and the Last Man.* London: Penguin.

Gardner, H. (1984) *Frames of Mind: The theory of multiple intelligences.* London: Fontana Press.

Goleman, D. (2002) *Emotional Intelligence.* New York: Bantam Books.

Gordon, W. H. H. US Creativity Guru. http://creatingminds.org/quoters/quoters_g.htm [accessed 17th November 2008]

Huxtable, M. (2003) 'The Elasticated Learner: Beyond curriculum learning opportunities in a local authority'. *Gifted Education International,* Vol.17 No.2.

Hymer, B. (2007) How do I understand and communicate my values and beliefs in my work as an educator in the field of giftedness? D.Ed.Psy. University of Newcastle. Available from http://www.actionresearch.net/hymer.shtml [accessed 11th October 2008]

Hymer, B. J. & Michel, D. (2002) *Gifted and Talented Learners: Creating a policy for inclusion.* London: NACE/David Fulton Publishers.

Ikeda, D. (2004) *A Piece of Mirror and Other Essays.* Kuala Lumpar: Soka Gakkai Malaysia.

Jeffries, M. & Hancock, T. (2002) *Thinking Skills: A teacher's guide.* Leamington Spa: Hopscotch.

Kellett, M. (2005) *How to Develop Children as Researchers: A step-by-step guide to teaching the research process.* London: Paul Chapman Publishing.

Kerry, T. (1998) *Questioning and Explaining in Classrooms.* London: Hodder and Stoughton.

Lather, P. (1991) *Getting Smart: Feminist research and pedagogy within the postmodern.* New York: Routledge.

Lipman, M. (2003) *Thinking in Education.* Cambridge: Cambridge University Press.

Maree, K. (ed) (2007) *Shaping the Story: A guide to facilitating narrative career counselling.* Pretoria: Van Schaik Publishers.

Mallett, M. (1999) *Young Researchers: Informational reading and writing in the early years and primary years.* London: Routledge.

McGuinness, C. (1999) *From Thinking Skills to Thinking Classrooms: A review and evaluation of approaches for developing pupils' thinking.* London: DfEE (Research Report RR115). http://www.dfes.gov.uk/research/data/uploadfiles/RB115.doc [accessed 11th October 2008]

McNiff, J. (2007) 'My Story is My Living Educational Theory', in Clandinin, J. (2007) *Handbook of Narrative Inquiry: Mapping a Methodology.* London: Sage Publications.

Medawar, P. B. (1969) *Induction and Intuition in Scientific Thought.* London: Methuen & Co. Ltd.

Mounter, J. (2008) 'Can children carry out action research about learning, creating their own learning theory?' *Gifted Education International,* Vol.24, pp.204-212.

Mounter, J. (2008) 'How can I enhance the educational influence of my pupils in their own learning, that of other pupils, myself and the school?' *Masters Educational Inquiry*, University of Bath. http://www.actionresearch.net/mastermod.shtml [accessed 19th October 2008]

Mpemba, E. B. (1979) 'The Mpemba Effect', *Physics Education (Institute of Physics)* 14: 410–412.

Mpemba, E. B. & Osborne, D. G. (1969) 'Cool?', *Physics Education (Institute of Physics)* 4:172–175.

Pratchett, T. (2006) *Hogfather*. London: Corgi.

Quinn, V. (1997) *Critical Thinking in Young Minds*. London: David Fulton Publishers.

Renzulli, J. & Reis, S. (1985) *The Schoolwide Enrichment Model: A how-to guide for educational excellence*. Mansfield Center, CT: Creative Learning Press.

Shekerjian, D. (1990) *Uncommon Genius*. New York: Penguin.

Sternberg, R. J. (1996) *Successful Intelligence*. New York: Plume.

Wallace, B. (ed) (2001) *Teaching Thinking Skills Across the Primary Curriculum*. London: David Fulton Publishers.

Wallace, B., Maker, J., Cave, D. & Chandler, S. (2004) *Thinking Skills and Problem-solving: An inclusive approach*. London: David Fulton Publishers.

West, T. G. (1997) *In the Mind's Eye*. New York: Prometheus Books.

Whitehead, J. & McNiff, J. (2006) *Action Research: Living Theory*. London: Sage Publications.

Whitehead, J. (1989) 'Creating a Living Educational Theory from Questions of the Kind, How Do I Improve My Practice?' *Cambridge Journal Of Education*, Vol.19, No.1, 1989, pp.41-52.

Winslade, J. (2007) Chapter 4: Constructing a career narrative through the care of self, pp.52-62 in Maree, K. (ed) (2007) *Shaping the Story: A guide to facilitating narrative career counselling*. Pretoria: Van Schaik Publishers.

Wood, D. (2nd ed) (1997) *How Children Think and Learn*. London: Blackwell.

Resources

Buzan, T. (2003) *Mind Maps for Kids*. London: Thorsons

This book is a good, colourful introduction to using Mind Maps with young children. His work is well known and a quick introduction can be found on his website www.buzanworld.com/Mind_Maps.htm

Claxton, G. & Luca, B. (2004) *Be Creative: Essential steps to revitalizing your work and life*. London: BBC Books.

Guy Claxton provides an entertaining and informative introduction to creative thinking with strategies to try yourself and will want to introduce with your pupils. Further details of his work can be found on www.guyclaxton.com

De Bono, E. (1985) *Six Hat Thinking*. London: Penguin.

This is a really easy read and you can get straight into using one of his best known thinking approaches. It is used widely in schools and business internationally. Edward De Bono has produced numerous books on thinking tools and strategies and ways of teaching thinking skills, all of which can be found on his website www.edwdebono.com

Fisher, R. (1996) *Stories for Thinking*. Oxford Nash Pollock: Publishing

Robert Fisher has produced many excellent books of stories, poems, games etc to use with children of many ages, including early years. His work on creative and philosophical thinking, for instance 'Teaching Children to Think', is inspirational. Details of his books for children and educators are on his website, which also has web resources on introducing and developing creative and philosophical thinking and an introduction to 'personalised research'. www.teachingthinking.net

Fleetham, M. (2007) *Thinking Stories to Wake up your Mind*. Cambridge: LDA.

Stories you can use with children. Mike Fleetham has other books, including the one he co-authored on Daily Brain Teasers for 7-9 year olds, and other materials you can look at on his website www.thethinkingclassroom.co.uk

Kellett, M. (2005) *How to Develop Children as Researchers: A Step-by-Step Guide to Teaching the Research Process*. London: Paul Chapman Publishing.

Mary Kellett, Founding Director of the Children's Research Centre at the Open University, guides the reader through developing formal social science research with children 10-14 years of age with practical examples. Further details of Mary Kellett's work and the work of the Children's Research Centre can be found on http://childrens-research-centre.open.ac.uk/

Perkins, D. (1995) *Smart schools: Better Thinking and Learning for Every Child*. New York: Simons & Schuster.

David Perkins, co-director of Harvard Project Zero, is very engaging writer. Enjoyed this book as a readable introduction to thoughtful learning, taking the reader from the theory to practice including issues to do with developing the curriculum, the classroom and the school and beyond. American but very pertinent to English context. More about his work on www.pz.harvard.edu/PIs/DP.htm

Video clips of him talking about his work on www.ltscotland.org.uk/learningaboutlearning/aboutlal/biogs/biogdavidperkins.asp

Potter, M. (2007) Outside the Box 7-9. London: A&C Black

Molly Potter has produced many books of ideas to be used with children of different ages. Great resource.

Wallace, B. (ed.) (2001) *Teaching Thinking Skills Across the Primary Curriculum: A practical approach for all abilities*. London: A NACE/David Fulton Publication.

Belle Wallace has many books with practical examples of the use of TASC (Thinking Actively in a Social Contexts) in primary classrooms and how it can be used to engage children of different ages in thinking as an inquiry and through the curriculum, for instance history. You will find TASC referenced on the DCSF standards site. Visit the NACE (National Association for Able Children in Education) website www.nace.co.uk/tasc/tasc_home.htm and a useful introduction and free online resource on http://etasc.londongt.org

Whitehead, J. & McNiff, J. (2006) *Action Research, Living Theory*. London: Sage Publications.

This book and others by Jack Whitehead and Jean McNiff provide an introduction to action research and living theory. Both have websites where you will find extensive resources and teachers accounts of their developing classroom practice. There is something for everyone, from those new to researching to improve what you do to those who are working on their doctorates. www.actionresearch.net and www. jeanmcniff.com

Wray, D. & Lewis, M. (1997) *Extending Literacy: Children reading and writing non-fiction*. London: Routledge.

'Does eating nettles prickle a caterpillar's tongue?' How do you help children extend their thinking by researching their question? A very good read which introduces writing frames and other strategies for engaging children thoughtfully with non-fiction.

David Wray is now Professor of Literacy Education at the University of Warwick and further details of his work and resources can be found on www.warwick.ac.uk/staff/D.J.Wray/

Websites

SAPERE is an educational charity whose members are interested in the role of philosophical inquiry in education, both as a model of rigorous thinking and as a celebration of wonder and open-mindedness. The website offers a guide to Philosophy for Children, resources, newsletters, links to other P4C sites and lots more and you can find out where their courses are running, which you will find invaluable whether you decide to run dedicated P4C sessions with the children, want to improve your classroom skills and/or develop a community which inquires together. http://sapere.org.uk/

Dip a toe into the wider waters of philosophical thinking internationally, inter-culturally and in the secondary citizenship agenda by visiting 'Thinking Worlds'. www.thinkingworlds.org

The Society for Philosophical Inquiry has a guide for starting and facilitating a philosophers' club with children and resources you might like to explore to extend your own philosophical thinking. www.philosopher.org/en/Home.html

The Mantle of the Expert has resources and material to develop an imaginative-inquiry approach to learning in the classroom. www.mantleoftheexpert.com

The DCSF standards web site has a lot of material that provides reading to extend your thinking about 'Thinking'. www.standards.dfes.gov.uk/thinkingskills

QCA has a lot of material on thinking skills in different places on the site www.qca.org.uk/qca_1841.aspx

http://curriculum.qca.org.uk/key-stages-1-and-2/learning-across-the-curriculum/creativity/whatiscreativity/index.aspx

It is also helpful to know what your pupils are going onto so do have a look at 'Creativity and Critical thinking – for Key stages 3 -4'.

Teachernet is continually expanding. You might like to start with this, 'Nurturing creativity in young people', www.teachernet.gov.uk/docbank/index.cfm?id=11270

This section of the 'Learning about Teaching Scotland' website has views from leading thinkers including movie clips and further reading.

www.ltscotland.org.uk/learningaboutlearning/aboutlal/biogs/index.asp

Futurelab is a not-for-profit organisation working in partnership with the creative, technology and educations sectors to develop material, resources and projects with latest thinking on creative learning and educational IT. Lots to explore. www.futurelab.org.uk

Inquiring minds is an approach to teaching and learning developed by Futurelab; projects to get involved, resources to download and papers to read. www.enquiringminds.org.uk/

There are many videos commercially produced that are excellent for stimulating a philosophical discussion. Disney's 'Cars' and 'Jungle Book', for instance, offer endless opportunities for philosophical discussions with young children as the format is often a 'good' v 'evil'.

Bloom's Taxonomy

Knowledge

Defined as – recalling, remembering

Teacher – tells, shows…

Activity – concept mapping…

Questions – what do you know about…?

Comprehension

Defined as – grasping the meaning

Teacher – listens, questions…

Activities – draw a picture…

Questions – can you give another example?

Application

Defined as – using information to solve a new problem

Teacher – facilitates, critically appraises

Activities – teach, report…

Questions – can you demonstrate?

Analysis

Defined as – breaking into constituent parts, detecting relationships…

Teacher – guides…

Activities – how does this relate?

Synthesis

Defined as – restructuring parts into something new

Teacher – reflects, extends

Activities – compare, generalise

Questions – devise, invent

Evaluation

Defined as – making judgements about value for purpose

Teacher – clarifies…

Activities – debate, rate…

Questions – is this the best way?

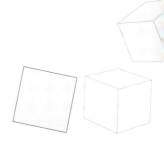